50

ADVENTURES

TO HAVE BEFORE

you turn 14

Pierdomenico Baccalario
Tommaso Percivale
Illustrated by AntonGionata Ferrari

sourcebooks
jabberwocky

First published in the United States in 2019 by Sourcebooks, Inc.

Text © 2016, 2019 by Pierdomenico Baccalario and Tommaso Percivale
Cover and internal design © 2019 by Sourcebooks, Inc.
Cover art © 2019 by Tim Wesson
Illustrations © 2016 by AntonGionata Ferrari
Internal images © Freepik
Translated from Italian by Sara Hauber

Published by Sourcebooks Jabberwocky, an imprint of Sourcebooks, Inc.
P.O. Box 4410, Naperville, Illinois 60567-4410
(630) 961-3900
Fax: (630) 961-2168
sourcebooks.com

Originally published as *Il manuale delle 50 avventure da vivere prima dei 13 anni* in 2016 in Italy by Editrice il Castoro Srl. This edition issued based on the hardcover edition published in 2016 in Italy by Editrice il Castoro Srl.

Library of Congress Cataloging-in-Publication data is on file with the publisher.

Source of Production: Leo Paper, Heshan City, Guangdong Province, China.
Date of Production: January 2019
Run Number: 5013953

Printed and bound in China.
LEO 10 9 8 7 6 5 4 3 2 1

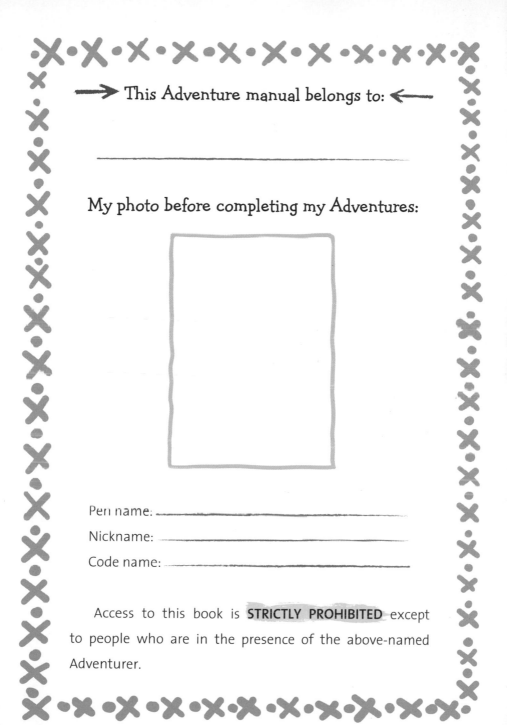

→ This Adventure manual belongs to: ←

_____

My photo before completing my Adventures:

Pen name: _____

Nickname: _____

Code name: _____

Access to this book is **STRICTLY PROHIBITED** except to people who are in the presence of the above-named Adventurer.

EXCEPTIONS

Only the following people may flip through the pages of this book:

1. _____

2. _____

3. _____

And, in case it ends up in the hands of evil villains, the following superheroes are also allowed to access this book:

1. _____

2. _____

3. _____

I began to tackle my Adventures on:
(MONTH/DAY/YEAR)

_____

at the age of _____ years,

and I completed all of the Adventures in this book on
(MONTH/DAY/YEAR)

_____

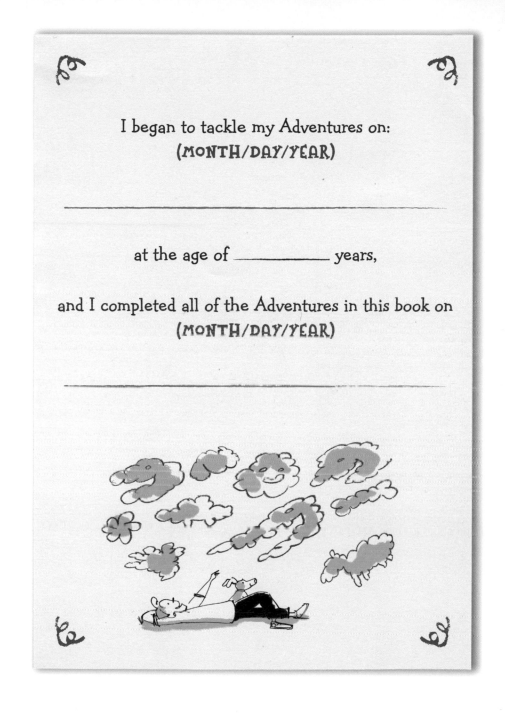

THE LAWS OF THIS BOOK

Hidden in the pages of this book are many treasures. No one can steal these treasures from you once you find them—they are yours forever. These treasures might seem small, totally normal, or even uninteresting to you now. It's hard to put a value on them. But in time, you'll notice them shining like diamonds in the sun.

All treasure hunters follow one simple (but ancient) rule: have fun!

Every time you open this book, you should be ready to have an unforgettable day.

Are you ready?

RULES FOR USING THIS BOOK

1. Bring this book with you everywhere. Any moment could be the right time to complete one of your Adventures.
2. Be sure to respect these rules.
3. If you don't like these rules, cross them out and invent new ones.
4. Begin your Adventures only after you have signed the Adventurers' Contract.
5. You can write, draw, or doodle on every page of this book, including the cover.
6. You are also authorized to damage this book. You can mark it up, drench it in water, rip out pages, chew on it, or tape over pages in the course of your Adventures. You can attach photos, tickets, leaves, feathers, and anything else you want. This book will live with you—facing every challenge you face without turning around and backing out.
7. From now on, you have to jump on one leg.
8. Rule #7 is no longer valid.
9. You must complete as many Adventures as possible.
10. For every Adventure that you complete, assign it a score from 1 to 10 in answer to the following questions, 1 meaning not very much and 10 meaning a lot: How much courage did you need? How much did you learn? How much fun did you have?
11. Add up the points to arrive at a total value for each Adventure.
12. If an Adventure requires that an adult be present, you absolutely

must complete that Adventure with an adult. Otherwise, that Adventure can't be counted as completed.

13. There isn't a #13 because that number brings bad luck.

14. The best way to have fun with this book is to complete your Adventures with friends.

ADVENTURERS' CONTRACT

(To Be Read Out Loud in Front of Two Witnesses and Once More in Front of a Mirror)

I, the undersigned (first and last name)

_____

to the best of my physical and mental abilities, accept the challenge to be an Adventurer and agree to the following:

I solemnly swear to commit myself to completing the Adventures presented in this book.
I solemnly swear that I will have fun.
I solemnly swear that I will share my Adventures with any and all friends who ask to join me.
I solemnly swear to respect the laws of this book.

Sincerely,

_____

THE ESSENTIALS

Adventure isn't a joke. Adventurers know this, so they make sure to always carry adequate equipment. Such equipment might cost very little, but it must be selected with the utmost care and attention.

The following are things that you must not forget to pack in your pockets or backpack as you explore the world:

STRING: Either packing string or cooking string is fine. Bring one or two arms (a unit of measure equal to the length of your arm) of string with you on all Adventures. Professional Adventurers use mountain climbers' cord (available in various colors and thicknesses), or parachute cord, which is the synthetic cord that parachutists use that can support up to 550 pounds. If you have a little extra savings, you can buy some parachute cord at a large sporting goods store or a hunting/outdoors store.

PENCIL: Any pencil is fine, as long as it's sharpened. A permanent marker is fine too, but you'll need to check it often to make sure it's not dried out. If you need to draw lines on pavement or cement (for example, for playing marbles), you can use a piece of colored chalk.

LIGHTER OR MATCHES: Fire is one of the most useful things there is. Learn how to understand and respect it, and it will respect you. You will need some fire to burn synthetic cord after you've cut

it so that the ends don't fray. If you prefer, you can bring a box of matches rather than a lighter. Ask your parents where to get some. Adults must ALWAYS be present when you're using these tools.

SWISS ARMY KNIFE: After early human beings learned to tame fire, they needed to find something to cut with. They made arrowheads and utensils by sharpening rocks. Nowadays, you can simply buy a multiuse Swiss Army knife that has things like a bottle opener (for your root beer), tweezers, and other useful tools, all folded into a pocket-size package. A basic model costs less than ten dollars, and you can find one at most supermarkets or hardware stores. You should only use a Swiss Army knife with an adult present.

MAGNIFYING GLASS: If Sherlock Holmes had one, then everyone must have one—not only for seeing things up close and in detail, but also for lighting fires in an emergency (although doing that is not as easy as they say it is). This, however, should only be done with adult supervision. You can find a magnifying glass in a craft store. But before you go buy one, make sure you don't already have one in the house (or perhaps your grandparents' house).

CANDY: These little pieces of sugar are indispensable for surviving the more tricky Adventures you'll encounter. But remember the ancient rule to always hide your candy  from bigger kids. It will be useful to you on many occasions.

ADHESIVE TAPE: It doesn't matter what kind, even though the transparent kind you use at school might be a little fragile. Electrical tape is better because it is fire resistant and slightly elastic. You might also try some strong gaffer's tape or duct tape.

FLASHLIGHT: Use this for seeing in the dark and at dusk. Remember to bring extra batteries!

WATCH: If you can, choose a watch that charges automatically or from solar power. It should also be shock resistant.

CELL PHONE: Adventurers typically don't like cell phones because they don't like to always be reachable. But a cell phone can be quite useful—especially a smartphone with apps.

The following are not essential for your Adventures, but they might be useful:

MARBLES: You can start a game anywhere there is adequate space. Plus, it's a very old game—a very, very old game. And Adventurers LOVE old things.

A LITTLE NOTEBOOK: For jotting down things that come to mind when you're away from home.

But the most important thing you must always have with you is, of course, this book.

THE 50 ADVENTURES

ADVENTURE #1

FEED AT LEAST SEVEN DIFFERENT ANIMALS

Animals are usually happy to eat any time, any place, as long as the food is tasty. The difficult part of this Adventure is not actually feeding the animals—it's finding the different animals to feed!

Cats and dogs are pretty much everywhere, but do you know where to find a rabbit? A fish? A horse? County fairs usually feature cool and interesting kinds of animals like sheep, cows, and baby chicks, and petting zoos sometimes offer the opportunity to feed some of their residents. Your friends might even have some unusual pets! Just make sure you're not trying to approach

animals in the wild. Animals that aren't used to humans can be unpredictable and possibly dangerous. Even when you're dealing with domesticated animals, always remember to be careful because all animals are still, well, animals! They might accidentally bite your hand while they're trying to grab the food you're offering or jump up a little too enthusiastically. They're not trying to be mean. They're probably just really excited to eat!

There's one more important thing to know before you start this Adventure: choosing the food you'll offer your animals is as important as approaching them with care.

Some food that we humans love is actually poisonous to animals. Did you know that you should never feed domestic animals bread, pasta, or candy? Also, chocolate, grapes, and raisins are really dangerous for both cats and dogs, and avocados are harmful to parrots. Before you start feeding an animal, make sure the animal can safely eat what you're offering.

✔ MISSION ACCOMPLISHED!

I fed the following animals:

1. _____
2. _____
3. _____
4. _____
5. _____
6. _____
7. _____

🏆 MY POINTS FOR THIS ADVENTURE:

(score each category from 1 to 10)

Courage: _____

Curiosily/interest: _____

Care/attention: _____

Success/achievement: _____

Fun: _____

📖 RECOMMENDED READING:

The One and Only Ivan
by Katherine Applegate

📖 WHAT YOU'LL REMEMBER MOST ABOUT THIS ADVENTURE:

The good feeling that comes from nourishing something, the looks in the animals' eyes, the warm nuzzles and friendly licks of recognition, the scent of the animals, and the new friendships that you made.

ADVENTURE #2

STRAP ON SKATES AND GO SKATING

The wind that strikes your cheeks, the speed that messes up your hair, the street that slides quickly by, the crackling under your feet—when you're riding a bike, you can feel all of these sensations.

But what happens when, instead of being seated and using the pedals to turn the bike's wheels, you have to rely on your own strength and balance to propel yourself forward? What happens when the wheels, instead of rolling in front of and behind you, are attached to your feet? Do you feel the same emotions, or are they even stronger? Are you more scared or less?

Wagons, bikes, cars, and

even airplanes use wheels for transporting people and things. But wheels can also let you feel like you're flying without wings as you race through the streets and sidewalks of your town.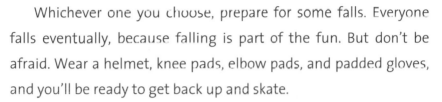

You can try classic roller skates or a skateboard for this Adventure.

Whichever one you choose, prepare for some falls. Everyone falls eventually, because falling is part of the fun. But don't be afraid. Wear a helmet, knee pads, elbow pads, and padded gloves, and you'll be ready to get back up and skate.

In many places, skating rinks feature supersmooth pavement or wooden floors where you can enjoy skating inside, even when it's raining. They are perfect for learning because you can rent skates and also take part in classes for beginners.

When you get good enough to go faster, you can try your hand at some tricks that test your abilities. In some cities, skate parks are even outfitted with special skating obstacles. Now get skating!

✔ MISSION ACCOMPLISHED!

🏆 MY POINTS FOR THIS ADVENTURE:

(score each category from 1 to 10)

Courage: _____

Curiosity/interest: _____

Care/attention: _____

Success/achievement: _____

Fun: _____

RECOMMENDED READING:

Dorothy's Derby Chronicles
by Meghan Dougherty
and Alece Birnbach

WHAT YOU'LL REMEMBER MOST ABOUT THIS ADVENTURE:

The speed, the adrenaline, your heart leaping over each obstacle, the impact of the earth each time you fell, and the feeling of pure happiness because, after you fell, you realized that you always got back up.

ADVENTURE #3

PLAY SOCCER OUTDOORS

What is it that makes soccer the world's most popular sport? The running, the footwork, the fact that anyone can play it anywhere, indoors or outdoors? The simple rules, the company of friends, the fact that competition takes a back seat to the fun and the sweat at the end of the game?

It is all of those things together, perhaps, and many more. Soccer is a simple sport to play: you only need a ball (which can really be made of anything from leather to a ball of old socks) and...well, your feet.

We don't need to explain the rules of soccer to you—or

maybe we do. You have to kick the ball into the opposing team's goal, behind their goalie. The goalie is the only player who can use their hands, but they can only do so in the area that is close to the team's goal. The other players can use any part of your body to touch the ball except for their arms and hands. In the end, whoever gets the most goals wins the game.

You just need to recruit some friends (at least two, but more friends means more fun) and find an open space to play. Any space will do—from your driveway to a nearby park. A grassy field helps you not get hurt when you fall, but it's not required.

To build a standard goal:

You don't necessarily need to mark the boundaries of the soccer field, but you can't play soccer unless the goals on each end are clearly marked. If you have nothing else, you can always use two backpacks to mark the sides of the goal or two rolled-up sweat-shirts. The best thing, though, would be to use two wooden posts stuck into the ground to mark the goal's boundaries. If you want to really do it right, put up a crossbar to mark the upper limit of the goal. Creating a goal like this takes some work. It's not enough to simply lay a stick across the tops of the two poles that mark the goal's boundaries, because at the slightest hit, the stick would fall on your head. Instead, you'll need to build the goal with some care.

First and foremost, consider the measurements of the goal. A regulation-size goal is 7.32 meters (24 feet) long by 2.44 meters (8 feet) high. But those are measurements for adult players. Instead, let's say that your goal should be about five strides wide and a little taller than you are when you stand on your toes with your arms above your head. Make sense?

At this point, you'll need to find three posts: two shorter ones, each split like a "Y" at the top, to drive into the ground and serve as side posts, and one longer one to lay horizontally across the tops of the two side posts. This longer post serves as the crossbar or top of the goal box. You'll need to affix it securely to the side posts using your string.

And now, it's time to play!

✓ MISSION ACCOMPLISHED!

Below, write the names of everyone
who played soccer with you (divided by teams)
and the results of the games you played.

🏆 MY POINTS FOR THIS ADVENTURE:

(score each category from 1 to 10)

Courage: _____

Curiosity/interest: _____

Care/attention: _____

Success/achievement: _____

Fun: _____

RECOMMENDED READING:

Out of Bounds
by Andrea Montalbano

WHAT YOU'LL REMEMBER MOST ABOUT THIS ADVENTURE:

Sweating, using your hardworking muscles, your desire to score a goal, the great feeling of being part of a team, the encouraging cheers of your teammates, the desire to make a comeback after you lost a game, the games won at the very last second, and the cheers of the crowd rooting for you.

ADVENTURE #4

LEARN TO TIE FIVE KNOTS

Ropes can tie and untie, attach and release, haul, support, tighten, lift, wrap, untie, or separate. Without ropes, ships couldn't be steered, wooden bridges would fall down, nets wouldn't exist, and captured prisoners would escape in the blink of an eye.

The art of making and using ropes is ancient. Since primitive times, people understood that being able to connect one thing to another was as important to survival as food, sleep, and defending themselves from enemies. Understanding how to use a rope teaches you how to get by in lots of different situations.

There are a million different ways to tie ropes, and each one is appropriate in certain specific situations. We chose five of the simplest and most versatile knots that should prove very handy. To complete this Adventure, you have to learn to make all five.

THE SIMPLE KNOT:

This one has a thousand uses. It's the knot used to secure the thread to a sewing needle. It can also be used to create a rock climbing rope. Making a knot every half meter (1.64 feet) creates a rope with many grips.

THE SAVOY KNOT:

This is an enhanced version of the Simple Knot.

THE POLE KNOT:

This knot is used to connect a rope to a pole or post. Its big advantage over other knots is that when the rope is not under tension, it's very easy to untie the knot. This knot is also used for fastening flags or banners.

THE BOWLINE KNOT:

Use this knot to make a noose at the end of a rope. With it, you can catch something. Because of that, it's often used by rescuers as a lifeline.

THE SIMPLE SLIPKNOT:

Slipknots tighten around something when the rope is pulled. You can also make one by passing the rope through a bowline knot.

Get yourself a piece of string or a soft nylon cord and practice making and undoing these knots until you can do each of them with your eyes closed.

✓ MISSION ACCOMPLISHED!

Cut off a short piece of the rope you used and attach it here with tape.

🏆 MY POINTS FOR THIS ADVENTURE:

(score each category from 1 to 10)

Courage: _____

Curiosity/interest: _____

Care/attention: _____

Success/achievement: _____

Fun: _____

WHAT YOU'LL REMEMBER MOST ABOUT THIS ADVENTURE:

The concentration needed, the satisfaction of making a challenging knot, and the coarse surface of the rope that grated on your fingertips.

RECOMMENDED READING:

Knots in My Yo-yo String
by Jerry Spinelli

ADVENTURE #5

FLY A KITE

Humans have always dreamed of flying: launching into the air, the dizziness of being airborne, floating in the wide open skies...

For thousands of years, we have looked skyward and admired (and envied) birds, with their long and light feathers, their graceful takeoffs, and their ability to leave the world behind to find another high above where the wind pushes them even higher. For thousands of years, myths and legends have told of humans' desire to fly. But until the Wright brothers invented the airplane (1903), flying was only a daydream.

Still, there has always been a fun and safe way to give us the sensation of flying while keeping our feet on the ground: flying kites!

The best-known kites are diamond shaped, and these are also the easiest to make. But there are other shapes and types of kites, including many inexpensive ones. Choose one that works for you and find just the right place to launch it into the air. But remember: there must be wind to make it fly.

You could try the beach, a meadow, or you could go into the hills—preferably someplace with a great panoramic view.

To launch the kite into the air, you'll need to unfurl the string that's fastened to the spool and start to run, pulling the kite behind you until it rises off the ground.

✓ MISSION ACCOMPLISHED!

🏆 MY POINTS FOR THIS ADVENTURE:

(score each category from 1 to 10)

Courage: _____

Curiosity/interest: _____

Care/attention: _____

Success/achievement: _____

Fun: _____

WHAT YOU'LL REMEMBER MOST ABOUT THIS ADVENTURE:

The wind rushing past you, the tangled line of the kite, the feeling of being free as a bird high above, and the wind against the back of your kite.

RECOMMENDED READING:

The Kite Fighters by Linda Sue Park

ADVENTURE #6

IDENTIFY TEN CLOUDS

Finding shapes in cloud formations is a magical and imaginative experience that tells us a lot about our character and our dreams.

Clouds are a funny and fascinating meteorological phenomenon. They are formed by the wind like clay is formed between fingers, and they always take different forms just waiting to be interpreted by somebody like you.

To begin this Adventure, you should lie on your back outside (we recommend doing so in an open field or park because the soft grass will help you concentrate) and stay there with your nose in the air.

What do the clouds above you resemble? Is that one a rocket? Is that other one a fish with an old man's beard? Maybe even the face of your uncle Hank?

Find at least ten different forms. The weirder they are, the better.

✓ MISSION ACCOMPLISHED!

Draw the most bizarre cloud formations you found here (at least 3 of them):

🏆 **MY POINTS FOR THIS ADVENTURE:**

(score each category from 1 to 10)

Courage: ⎯⎯⎯⎯⎯⎯⎯

Curiosity/interest: ⎯⎯⎯⎯⎯⎯

Care/attention: ⎯⎯⎯⎯⎯⎯⎯

Success/achievement: ⎯⎯⎯⎯⎯

Fun: ⎯⎯⎯⎯⎯⎯⎯⎯⎯

RECOMMENDED READING:
The Neverending Story
by Michael Ende

WHAT YOU'LL REMEMBER MOST ABOUT THIS ADVENTURE:

The sensation of being limitless, the tickle of the grass on your neck, the scent of the sun warming your cheeks, the feeling of being disoriented after staring at the sky so long, and the disappointment of having to bring your thoughts back to earth.

ORGANIZE A TREASURE HUNT

Only one thing in the world is more fun than participating in a treasure hunt: creating one. To actually make up a puzzle or riddle requires a mind at least as brilliant as one used to solve it.

A treasure hunt consists of a sequence of clues that leads to the place where something special (the treasure, of course) is hidden. The clues should not be totally clear or obvious—they should be difficult enough to present a challenge, but not impossible for the participants to figure out.

The backdrop in which the treasure hunt takes place is important, but not too important. It's true that a medieval castle would be a lot more spectacular than a park, but your imagination can help you transform a regular place into someplace spectacular.

It's important that you know the location and its features well so you can create a treasure hunt that will stump your friends.

Usually the clues for a treasure hunt are written down for participants. For example, riddles or nursery rhymes are perfect, just like these two examples:

"The next clue you'll find where you can see the whole world in just a few seconds."

This could be a globe or a map (one that is hanging up, or at least visible).

"It's the only house that doesn't have a door."

This might be a birdhouse

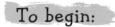

To begin:

Gather five sheets of paper and five envelopes and number them 1 through 5. Then spend some time studying the place where you want to hide the treasure. It must be a place that's easy to reach, but obviously not too easy to guess. Under the bed? Sure. Or rather, "Where the boogeyman hides." Describe this final hiding place in vague or cryptic language, write the number 5 at the top, and seal it in its envelope. Then, you'll need to find a good place to hide that clue. Your clues should not be hidden too close to one another. Make your treasure hunters work for it!

When you have found a good place to hide that final clue, get to work describing (remember to be cryptic!) where your hunters can find it on sheet #4, and keep repeating this process until you've sealed envelope #1, which is the first clue you'll hand to your treasure hunters.

The hunters should then find each hidden envelope, one after the other, and follow each clue until they find the final treasure.

The more effort you put into organizing the hunt, the more fun it will be.

The treasure:

The treasure that you hide isn't the most important part of the game. The key to a good treasure hunt is...the hunt!

However, if you don't offer something kind of special at the end of the game, you'll have a group of tired, disappointed friends to answer to.

Want some advice? You could hide a board game that all of you could play together, a video game, or a good book. And remember to attach a message for the winning hunters—some kind of certificate of achievement that they can keep forever, written especially for them. That will be the best treasure of all.

✓ MISSION ACCOMPLISHED!

Attach here (folded up) the clue that was the hardest for your treasure hunters to figure out.

🏆 MY POINTS FOR THIS ADVENTURE:

(score each category from 1 to 10)

Courage: _____

Curiosity/interest: _____

Care/attention: _____

Success/achievement: _____

Fun: _____

RECOMMENDED READING:

Treasure Island
by Robert Louis Stevenson

WHAT YOU'LL REMEMBER MOST ABOUT THIS ADVENTURE:

The hours you spent racking your brains to come up with the best possible puzzle (and then afterward seeing your friends rack their brains to solve it), the urge to give them hints during the hunt, and the collaboration between the hunters.

MAKE A GIGANTIC SOAP BUBBLE

Think of something that exists but doesn't exist, that has a body but doesn't weigh anything, that is closed but transparent, that is colorless but contains all colors, that is extremely fragile but its fragility allows it to travel long distances.

You're thinking about a soap bubble. Soap bubbles are magical. And if you think it's challenging to make small ones, well...try to make big ones. It's a serious challenge!

To complete this Adventure, you need to make absolutely gigantic soap bubbles—so gigantic that you can fit inside of them!

The recipe:

Gather these ingredients:

- 1 cup of dish soap
- ½ cup of water
- ⅓ cup of liquid glycerin (which you can find at a drugstore)
- 2 teaspoons of powdered sugar

1. Mix everything in a bucket. Mix slowly so you don't create too many soap suds.
2. Cover it with a lid and let it rest for a day or two.
3. Then, to make the size of bubble you want to make, you need a large ring. You can make one by shaping a metal shirt hanger—the kind they use at the dry cleaners—into a circle. Dip the ring into the special liquid you mixed, lift it close to your face, and blow all the air out of your lungs! If your breath isn't enough to fill the bubble, you can gently wave the soapy ring right to left. It will fill with air and blow itself up until it's full.

 MISSION ACCOMPLISHED!

Let a drop of your special soapy liquid fall on the page and let it dry before closing the book.

MY POINTS FOR THIS ADVENTURE:

(score each category from 1 to 10)

Courage: _____

Curiosity/interest: _____

Care/attention: _____

Success/achievement: _____

Fun: _____

RECOMMENDED READING:

Bad Kitty Gets a Bath
by Nick Bruel

WHAT YOU'LL REMEMBER MOST ABOUT THIS ADVENTURE:

The scent of the soap, the delicate movements of the bubbles, the surprise, the colors, the swarms of bubbles floating through the air, the little squirts of soapy water on your nose—and your dad asking where on earth his shirt hanger went.

ADVENTURE #9

CLIMB A TREE

Some people climb trees to pick fruit. Some do it so they can get a great panoramic view from up high. The truth is you don't need a reason to climb a tree—you can do it just because it's fun to climb.

Your technique will evolve with experience, but here are some tips for your first time after you've gotten an adult's approval: As you climb, you should always have three points of contact with the tree. When you reach out a hand to grab a higher branch, your other hand should be tightly holding some other part of the tree, and your feet should be securely planted as well.

Don't jump. Ever.

And don't try to climb in slippers or in shoes that have a smooth sole. The best shoes for climbing are hiking boots!

✔ MISSION ACCOMPLISHED!

Gently pluck a leaf from the highest branch that you reached during your climb and tape it here.

🏆 MY POINTS FOR THIS ADVENTURE:

(score each category from 1 to 10)

Courage: _____

Curiosity/interest: _____

Care/attention: _____

Success/achievement: _____

Fun: _____

RECOMMENDED READING:

My Side of the Mountain by Jean Craighead George

WHAT YOU'LL REMEMBER MOST ABOUT THIS ADVENTURE:

The world seen from a new vantage point, your hands tight around the rough bark, the branches that creaked under your feet, the leaves that tickled your face and filled the space around you, the thrill and fear of being up so high, and how amazing it is to finally be at the top of the world.

ADVENTURE #10

BUILD A TREE HOUSE

When you're climbing a tree for Adventure #9, look around. Is it a sturdy tree? Maybe an oak with big, gnarled branches that fan out wide?

If it is, you've already found the perfect place to build a tree house.

However, to build your tree house, you can't just find a wooden table and a handful of nails. You need the help of an adult who knows how to use them. If your parents (or an adult you trust) has a garage with the right tools, ask them to help you. Building the tree house together will be an unforgettable experience, and it's not important if the result isn't perfect.

You can make a climbing rope—explained in Adventure #4, the Simple Knot—to help you reach your finished tree house easier, and you can use this opportunity to learn how to use some simple building tools.

Now that you have built your hideout, how will you use it? You could let yourself lounge in the breeze between the branches, reading a book in peace and quiet, in the shade of your very own refuge. You also could get to know your new neighbors—get some binoculars and scan the leaves for nests and birds singing melodic songs. You decide!

 MISSION ACCOMPLISHED!

🏆 MY POINTS FOR THIS ADVENTURE:

(score each category from 1 to 10)

Courage: _____

Curiosity/interest: _____

Care/attention: _____

Success/achievement: _____

Fun: _____

WHAT YOU'LL REMEMBER MOST ABOUT THIS ADVENTURE:

The thrill of being up high, the excitement of having your own private nest, and the desire to never climb down.

RECOMMENDED READING:

Song of the Trees
by Mildred D. Taylor

ADVENTURE #11

SLEEP IN A SCARY PLACE

Are you afraid of the dark? Of bugs? Of water?

Take your fears, lock them in a drawer, and throw away the key. To complete this Adventure, you have to sleep in a place that frightens you.

You don't have to go alone though. Friends and parents can accompany you. But the place you choose must be really special and dangerous.

For example, have you ever slept outdoors in a tent or sleeping bag? If you've never tried it, try sleeping first in your living room. Then, put your tent or sleeping bag on the porch or in your lawn. Finally, try it out in a nearby forest. When you're totally immersed in the dark of night, at first it will seem like you don't hear anything—not a peep. But as soon as you relax, you'll start to hear the voices of the world around you: the rattle of the trees quivering in the breeze, the incessant chirping of the cicadas and crickets, or the buzz of the electric cables stretching from one electrical pole to another (if you're near a street). You'll discover that when you sleep outside, your senses change. It feels like you have a thousand ears and a thousand noses, all of them as alert as antennae.

The night is long...

You're far from your bedroom, in a dark and isolated place, with a group of courageous friends. How will you pass the time? Obviously, you'll tell ghost stories!

You can take inspiration from the many books that recount tales of ghosts, werewolves, and witches. You can even invent your own. There's only one rule: the stories should also scare you!

✓ MISSION ACCOMPLISHED!

Write down all of the things that
made you scared during your wild
camping Adventure...

...and don't leave anything out!

🏆 MY POINTS FOR THIS ADVENTURE:

(score each category from 1 to 10)

Courage: _____

Curiosity/interest: _____

Care/attention: _____

Success/achievement: _____

Fun: _____

RECOMMENDED READING:

The Jungle Book
by Rudyard Kipling

WHAT YOU'LL REMEMBER MOST ABOUT THIS ADVENTURE:

The feeling of being part of a grand mystery, your aching back, the secret sounds of the night, the little sleep you got, and your friends' eyes shining brightly in the dark.

ADVENTURE #12

STUDY THE STARS

Look at the sky. What do you see? If there are no clouds and the night is still, see how the surface of the sky is dotted with stars.

Stars are always there, and they've been there since before we—or even our planet—came to be. Since the beginning of time, anyone could lift their gaze to the sky at night and see an immense expanse of little glowing lights—far away like a mirage, but reassuring like old friends. Stars are so reliable, in fact, that sailors still use them today to help them navigate. Try it yourself.

We'll give you some help: pick out Ursa Major (the Big

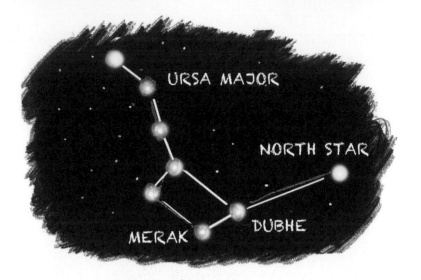

Bear), which contains the Big Dipper. Ursa Major is a constellation, which means it's a group of stars that make a figure when connected by straight lines. Finding a constellation is a little like playing the game "connect the dots," but without the numbers. Ursa Major looks like an old wagon without wheels, and the Big Dipper looks like a frying pan.

When you've found the outline of this constellation, try to pick out the final two stars—the ones that make the back of the "frying pan." These stars are called Merak and Dubhe. Draw an imaginary line between those two and then keep following it. The North Star is found exactly along this line, about four times as far as the distance between Merak and Dubhe.

There are eighty-eight total constellations up above you, and each one takes up a part of the sky. If you can, get an astronomy book (from your home, your school, or the library) or ask your parents to download an app that describes the constellations and try to identify at least five of them in the sky.

The most famous ones (other than Ursa Major) are Orion (which you can see in the winter), Cygnus (the Swan), and Scorpius (the Scorpion).

 # MISSION ACCOMPLISHED!

Did you find some interesting shapes while gazing at the sky? A hippo, an umbrella, or a kite? Draw your personal constellation below and give it a name.

 ## MY POINTS FOR THIS ADVENTURE:

(score each category from 1 to 10)

Courage: _____

Curiosity/interest: _____

Care/attention: _____

Success/achievement: _____

Fun: _____

WHAT YOU'LL REMEMBER MOST ABOUT THIS ADVENTURE:

The feeling of being very, very small, the enchantment, and the sense of vertigo after looking at the stars so long in the black of the night.

RECOMMENDED READING:

Pi in the Sky by Wendy Mass

ADVENTURE #13

AN ADULT MUST BE PRESENT!

MAKE A WALKING STICK

Sometimes, walking can get tough—like when the incline is too steep, the trail is long, or difficult terrain leaves you unbalanced. In all of these cases, you could use a trusty friend: a real walking stick.

This stick won't just help you with walking. A walking stick can also be used to help build a stretcher, cross a ditch, or measure the depth of a stream.

The best types of wood for creating walking sticks are dogwood, ash, maple, locust, elderberry, and elm.

To build a good walking stick, go into the forest or a wooded area and find a branch that has already fallen. It should be straight and about as tall as you are. You should be able to easily grip it in your hand at just the right height. Don't find a branch that's too big—three-fourths of an inch (2 cm) in diameter should be just fine.

For the next part, make sure you have an adult to help guide you. Use a knife to shave the tip of the stick until it's pointy but still sturdy so it can handle being used on uneven terrain.

Then, clean the grip (on the other end of the stick) so it's free from bark and not rough. Run a blade along the length of the stick to get rid of all the knots and bumps.

Finally, hold a ruler up next to the stick and mark little notches on the stick with measurements so that the stick can serve as a ruler when you're away from home (and don't have your ruler). Then, carve your name and the year in which you made the stick into it.

Now all you need to do is take a long, adventurous journey!

✓ MISSION ACCOMPLISHED!

I found the perfect branch
for my walking stick here:

MY POINTS FOR THIS ADVENTURE:

(score each category from 1 to 10)

Courage: _____

Curiosity/interest: _____

Care/attention: _____

Success/achievement: _____

Fun: _____

WHAT YOU'LL REMEMBER MOST ABOUT THIS ADVENTURE:

The effort to make your walking stick, the differences between the various types of wood, and the journey you took.

RECOMMENDED READING:

Johnny Appleseed
by Steven Kellogg

ADVENTURE #14

GO FOR A WALK
UNDER THE COVER OF DARKNESS

Days are divided in two parts: the daytime, which is lit by the sun and dedicated to productive activities, and the nighttime, which is protected by the moon and reserved for parties or resting.

This is a real shame, because the night has so much to offer. Darkness and silence are friends of owls, thieves, and spies, but also of the courageous, the strong, and those hungry for mystery. Night is a vast territory of unknown hazards and dangers to be explored.

To complete this Adventure, you must take a walk after sunset. You can choose a path in your city or town—better yet, you can explore a rural area.

In the company of an adult and perhaps some friends, venture into the heart of things that one sees only when there isn't any light. Open your ears and try to recognize every sound. Breathe deeply and discover the scents of the night.

Remember to move slowly and be extra careful with your movements so you don't hurt yourself.

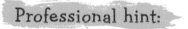
Professional hint:

Bring a flashlight with you, and don't forget to bring extra batteries so you don't get stuck in the dark.

✅ MISSION ACCOMPLISHED!

Record any sounds, smells, or encounters you had during your night of exploration here.

Sounds:

Smells:

Encounters:

🏆 MY POINTS FOR THIS ADVENTURE:

(score each category from 1 to 10)

Courage: _____

Curiosity/interest: _____

Care/attention: _____

Success/achievement: _____

Fun: _____

RECOMMENDED READING:

Animals at Night by Anne Jankéliowitch and Delphine Chedru

WHAT YOU'LL REMEMBER MOST ABOUT THIS ADVENTURE:

Your uncertain steps, the light from lampposts or the moon illuminating only certain parts of the ground, the night wrapped around you like a sweater, and the feeling that everything is a secret—everything, even you.

ADVENTURE #15

WATCH THE SUNRISE AND SUNSET ON THE SAME DAY

We see the transitions between day and night and take it for granted—but there is nothing more amazing. We owe everything to the sun. Without it, nothing around us would grow. There would be no grass, no trees, and no animals. There wouldn't even be rain, because without the evaporation of the sea and lakes, no clouds would exist.

To complete this Adventure, you need to watch the sunrise and sunset on the same day: greeting the sun as a tiny sliver of it peeks over the horizon, and then accompanying the sun again as it goes to sleep, setting over the opposite edge of the sky. Don't stare directly into the sun if it is shining brightly.

Here are some tips: The sun rises in the east and sets in the west. Therefore, find an observation point from which you can see both of these cardinal directions without any obstacles in the way. Also, the sunrise and sunset don't happen at the same times every day—they change based on the season. To learn the precise time that they'll happen, you can use any number of websites or a meteorological app. It's not necessary for you to stay awake the whole day—but if you want to undertake something really special, you could try to complete Adventures #11, #12, #14, and #15 in the same day!

✓ MISSION ACCOMPLISHED!

🏆 MY POINTS FOR THIS ADVENTURE:

(score each category from 1 to 10)

Courage: _____

Curiosity/interest: _____

Care/attention: _____

Success/achievement: _____

Fun: _____

WHAT YOU'LL REMEMBER MOST ABOUT THIS ADVENTURE:

The broad range of colors in the sky, the beams of light that danced on your skin, and the magic of a day being born and then dying. It certainly is a beautiful dream.

RECOMMENDED READING:

A Pizza the Size of the Sun by Jack Prelutsky and James Stevenson

ADVENTURE #16

PLANT YOUR OWN PLANT

This Adventure is not as easy as it sounds! But it will give you many secondary benefits, like having fresh basil leaves to put on your pizza.

Choose a plant or a flower to plant. If you don't have either a garden or a balcony, you can try to plant it on a windowsill. Keep in mind that not all plants can be planted at the same time of year. For example, basil is planted in late spring, between April and May.

You don't need to have a vase for your plant. A perforated plastic container like you see in supermarkets works just fine. However, you will need a little bit of compost or potting soil (which you can find at the supermarket or in any garden store).

Of course, you also need some seeds (and these are usually inexpensive).

Fill your container about halfway with potting soil. Sprinkle in the seeds, then cover them with another layer of soil. Next, you need to water them. If you can, use a spray bottle or a watering can instead of pouring water from a cup so that it falls in drops rather than in a heavy stream. Make sure to get all of the seeds wet.

Cover the container with a layer of plastic wrap. Remember to also put a plate under the container so that water won't leak onto the windowsill each time you water your seeds.

In the course of about a week, the first shoots will appear. As soon as you see them, remove the plastic wrap.

Slowly, the plants will continue to grow. Expose them to the sun, and don't forget to water them regularly. When the little plants are about 2 inches (5 cm) tall, pluck out and throw away the weakest ones (it's not worth it to try to make them grow—you can tell it's just not their time) and make it your goal to help the bigger ones grow even more robust.

✔ MISSION ACCOMPLISHED!

I planted this kind of plant:

_____

On this date:

_____

The first shoots appeared on this date:

_____

🏆 MY POINTS FOR THIS ADVENTURE:

(score each category from 1 to 10)

Courage: _____

Curiosity/interest: _____

Care/attention: _____

Success/achievement: _____

Fun: _____

WHAT YOU'LL REMEMBER MOST ABOUT THIS ADVENTURE:

The scent of the plants, the delicate shoots between your fingers, and the joy of seeing something grow thanks to your efforts.

RECOMMENDED READING:

The Secret Garden
by Frances Hodges Burnett

ADVENTURE #17

BUILD A SLINGSHOT

Slingshots are easy to build with simple materials that cost little to nothing at all—the hard part is learning to pull the slingshot and hit your mark.

To succeed in this Adventure, you have to do both of those things—build your slingshot and hit your mark—to show your skills in launching projectiles.

To build a proper slingshot, you need a smallish stick that splits at one end like the letter "Y." Look for one in a park, the woods, or your backyard.

The best wood comes from an oak tree, but any tough wood will do. You'll also need a piece of leather to make the grip, as well as a rubber band you can cut into two strips. If you don't have a big enough rubber band, you can also use a tourniquet (like the ones nurses use before giving you a shot in the arm) from the drugstore.

The grip (that is, the part in which the stone rests before you launch it) is a piece of leather big enough to allow, when folded in half, a rock as big as the tip of your thumb. It needs to have two punctures, one on each end, through which one strip of the elastic band will pass. You can get the leather from an old handbag or shoe (with your parents' permission).

When you have found the right piece of wood, strip it and clean it well. Then, you need to carve a thin space around the tips of the "Y" to create an indentation where you will tie one end of each of the elastic bands.

When the wood is clean, put it in the oven at almost four hundred degrees Fahrenheit. The heat from the oven will dry the wood's fibers, making it tougher. When the wood starts to change color and you start to smell its intense odor, take it out of the oven. Be careful not to burn yourself!

Now, let the wood cool, tightly tie one strip of the elastic at each end of the "Y," and attach the other ends of each piece to the small holes in each end of the grip (your strip of leather). Do this so that each of the elastic bands are the same length, or the slingshot won't shoot straight!

Once that's done, you can start to throw your stones—with caution! The slingshot should be held by your weaker hand and the elastic pulled back with your stronger hand. We strongly recommend wearing a glove on the hand that holds the slingshot,  because at first it's really easy to launch the stone right into your fingers. Also, wear a pair of protective glasses or goggles just in case the elastic strips snap.

Do a couple of practice rounds in a deserted location or against an old wall. Be careful to always pull the slingshot where it's safe to do so. You don't want to risk hurting yourself or someone else!

✔ MISSION ACCOMPLISHED!

🏆 MY POINTS FOR THIS ADVENTURE:

(score each category from 1 to 10)

Courage: _____

Curiosity/interest: _____

Care/attention: _____

Success/achievement: _____

Fun: _____

WHAT YOU'LL REMEMBER MOST ABOUT THIS ADVENTURE:

The possibility of hitting something far out of reach and the feel of holding something you created in your hands.

RECOMMENDED READING:

The Adventures of Tom Sawyer
by Mark Twain

HIT A TIN CAN AT TEN PACES

Now that you have your very own slingshot (built in Adventure #17), here's a way to use it. (You can also complete this Adventure with just your bare hands.)

Find a big, isolated place, preferably out in the country.

Take an empty tin can, stand it on a box, crate, or boulder (if you find one tall enough), and try to hit it from a distance of five steps away. Easy, right? Well, take five more steps away. Now it's a little more difficult.

Could you do it? Ah, beginner's luck. You can cross off this Adventure only after you've hit the can or jar five times in a row.

✅ MISSION ACCOMPLISHED!

🏆 MY POINTS FOR THIS ADVENTURE:

(score each category from 1 to 10)

Courage: _____

Curiosity/interest: _____

Care/attention: _____

Success/achievement: _____

Fun: _____

WHAT YOU'LL REMEMBER MOST ABOUT THIS ADVENTURE:

The missed shots, the soreness in your arms and shoulders, and your heart leaping when you hit your target.

RECOMMENDED READING:

The Summer Experiment
by Cathie Pelletier

ADVENTURE #19

ROLL DOWN A BIG HILL

All explorers seem to be drawn to high summits with views that take their breath away.

It's this type of view that inspires thousands of mountain climbers to risk their lives to reach the summit of Mount Everest: a fascinating, challenging, and dangerous mountain—and the tallest in the world.

To complete this Adventure, you don't need to go to Nepal or hire a team of Sherpas. Instead, find a tall hill in your area and climb up to the top. Climb all the way to the very highest point, nothing lower.

Now, enjoy the moment,

letting the view around you pierce you like an arrow. Close your eyes and breathe in the altitude.

Then, when it's time to descend, go down in style. Find a cleared slope or a field with a steep incline. It has to be a cleared, cleaned, empty space, free of stones and other debris. Check it well so you don't get hurt or end up in a pile of cow dung.

Finally, go to the top, stretch out on the ground with your arms extended overhead, your legs straight and squeezed together, let out a wild howl, and roll down the hill.

If you have friends with you, make it a race to see who can get down to the bottom first. Whoever wins will be at the head of the line during your next expedition.

✅ MISSION ACCOMPLISHED!

Record any injuries or
ruined clothing here:

🏆 MY POINTS FOR THIS ADVENTURE:

(score each category from 1 to 10)

Courage: _____

Curiosity/interest: _____

Care/attention: _____

Success/achievement: _____

Fun: _____

WHAT YOU'LL REMEMBER MOST ABOUT THIS ADVENTURE:

Seeing the vast, endless world, the butterflies in your stomach before you rolled down the hill, and your head as it spun and spun and spun.

RECOMMENDED READING:

Watership Down
by Richard Adams

ADVENTURE #20

TAKE PICTURES OF THREE WILD ANIMALS

A deer perks up its ears before drinking from a stream, listening for danger before letting down its guard. A robin flits in and out of a bush, gathering sticks to build its nest. A squirrel races down a tree and digs a hole in the ground, looking for nuts it stored before the winter.

These are all portraits of the animals that may live in nature around your house. To immortalize moments like these and capture images of animals in the wild, you need three things: a camera, a good observation point, and lots and lots of patience.

To complete this Adventure, you must find three wild animals and take pictures of them while staying hidden.

✔ MISSION ACCOMPLISHED!

I photographed the following animals:

🏆 MY POINTS FOR THIS ADVENTURE:

(score each category from 1 to 10)

Courage: _____

Curiosity/interest: _____

Care/attention: _____

Success/achievement: _____

Fun: _____

WHAT YOU'LL REMEMBER MOST ABOUT THIS ADVENTURE:

The excitement of anticipation, the waiting, the silence, the patience—and in some cases, the fear!

RECOMMENDED READING:

The Call of the Wild
by Jack London

ADVENTURE #21

FOLLOW TRACKS IN THE WOODS

Forests are living things. Different animals spend their lives there, driven by the natural rhythms of day and night. The search for food is the predominant drive that puts all animals, big and small, on the move. Rush hour in the forest occurs during the early evening and again close to dawn.

A trained eye can detect the signs that show animals have been on the move. Do you want to know whose tracks those are that get lost in the under-growth? Then throw yourself into this Adventure—and maybe also take the opportunity to complete Adventure #20!

Here's what to do: put on

boots that protect your ankles, thick socks, and long pants, then head out to a nearby forest and search through the undergrowth until you find some animal tracks.

If the tracks you find have a clearly defined outline and are pretty tidy, then they're fresh. Much depends on the moisture in the ground, but after a little while, the outlines of animals' tracks tend to get flattened out like a deflated balloon.

Here are illustrations of five animal tracks most commonly found in the woods:

SQUIRREL

DEER

FOX

RABBIT   HEDGEHOG

✓ MISSION ACCOMPLISHED!

I found the tracks of:

🏆 MY POINTS FOR THIS ADVENTURE:

(score each category from 1 to 10)

Courage: _____

Curiosity/interest: _____

Care/attention: _____

Success/achievement: _____

Fun: _____

RECOMMENDED READING:

The Wind in the Willows
by Kenneth Grahame

WHAT YOU'LL REMEMBER MOST ABOUT THIS ADVENTURE:

The curiosity and confusion, the intense scent of the earth and tree bark, the apparently random wandering of certain animals, and the mystery of nests and tracks that you couldn't quite make out.

ADVENTURE #22

AN ADULT MUST BE PRESENT!

BUILD A FIRE

If the wind is blowing, it's snowing, or we have feverish chills, we can simply turn up the heat in the house to make us feel better right away.

But when we are far from civilization—in the high plains of the Gobi Desert, on the trails of the Andes, or camping in the mountains—we need to go back to ancient, tried and true methods for getting warm.

Lighting a fire isn't only useful for warming us up. It's necessary for cooking, keeping animals away from camp, and giving us light at night when the moon isn't visible.

As an Adventurer, it is very useful to know how to light and put out a fire, as well as how to use and control fire.

To make a good fire, you have to prepare. Choose a sheltered place, protected from the wind. Clear the area of branches and dried leaves.

Next, form a circle made of stones and dig a small pit in the middle. This will be your hearth.

The most common fuel for a fire is wood. Wandering through the trees, you'll find many fallen and dried out trees that are perfect for your little fire. You'll need pieces of various sizes, from thin twigs to thicker branches (with the larger ones split into pieces).

To light the fire, you need some kindling, which is a small bunch of material that easily catches fire when lit. Straw works well, as do wood chips, leaves, sawdust (like that produced by woodworms), and also potato chips (yes, the kind in store-bought bags).

Build a little tepee of thin twigs and place the kindling in the center.

You can use one of several methods to light your fire. Lighters are the simplest to use (even survival experts use them), and so are matches. (A simple trick: you can let a small drop of candle wax drip onto each match head to make the matches water resistant, and thus usable even if they fall in water).

You can also use a magnifying glass. You have to tilt the glass in a way that concentrates the sun's rays at a single point on the kindling and stay there, not moving. After a little while, you'll see a thin line of smoke rising from the kindling. At that point, blow delicately on the kindling to help the fire really get started.

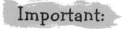

Important:

In many parts of the country, you're not allowed to light a fire. In some parks, you can find areas that are equipped for building campfires for cooking when it's allowed. Sometimes, the ban on building fires is limited to the summer season when the risk of a wildfire is greatest. Get informed about the rules in effect in the area you hope to build your fire before you get in big trouble.

✅ MISSION ACCOMPLISHED!

🏆 MY POINTS FOR THIS ADVENTURE:

(score each category from 1 to 10)

Courage: _____

Curiosity/interest: _____

Care/attention: _____

Success/achievement: _____

Fun: _____

> **RECOMMENDED READING:**
>
> *Hatchet* by Gary Paulsen

WHAT YOU'LL REMEMBER MOST ABOUT THIS ADVENTURE:

The feeling of giving new life to the ancient ritual of going into the woods and building a fire, choosing the branches to burn, preparing the hearth, the crackling of the newly-lit fire, and the warmth on your cheeks.

ADVENTURE #23

AN ADULT MUST BE PRESENT!

LEARN TO IDENTIFY MUSHROOMS

In the Paleolithic period—a period that happened a long, long time ago—no factories, offices, schools, or farms existed. People who lived in that era did not go to work, earn money, or go somewhere to buy food. So how did they survive?

Humans in that era were hunters and gatherers. That means that they scavenged through the forest looking for wild game and fruit (as well as wild flowers and berries) and they tried eating the things they found. Life was very fragile; all they needed was one day of bad luck, and they ended up going hungry.

Still today, there are

societies where this lifestyle of hunting and gathering is much the same.

You can try to imitate that way of life by learning to better understand the things in nature that you can eat —and which ones taste good! One example is mushrooms.

Mushrooms are unique. They are not considered a vegetable because they don't contain chlorophyll. Sometimes they get nourishment from organic materials that are decomposing. Sometimes they hit it off with a living tree and develop a symbiotic relationship, each nourishing the other.

Some types cling to humid corners in your house in the form of mildew, and some simply grow in fields, ready to be eaten. We're really only interested in identifying mushrooms though—not collecting them.

Here is a list of the most common types of mushrooms. Look for these in a forest and record what you find.

HONEY MUSHROOM

PORCINI MUSHROOM

OYSTER MUSHROOM

FIELD MUSHROOM

✓ MISSION ACCOMPLISHED!

I found the following mushrooms:

And the following treasures:

🏆 MY POINTS FOR THIS ADVENTURE:

(score each category from 1 to 10)

Courage: _____

Curiosity/interest: _____

Care/attention: _____

Success/achievement: _____

Fun: _____

RECOMMENDED READING:

The Borrowers by Mary Norton

WHAT YOU'LL REMEMBER MOST ABOUT THIS ADVENTURE:

The intense and musty scent of the mushrooms, the autumn soil that gave way under your feet, walking over a carpet of leaves, and the surprise when you found what you were looking for.

ADVENTURE #24

BUILD A SNOWMAN

Who doesn't enjoy rolling around on a bed covered by a big, soft down comforter? Well, the great outdoors has its own version of a fluffy cover that comes around while nature is sleeping during the winter months: snow! The best part is we can play with this soft blanket as much as we like.

After a winter snowstorm, make sure you're bundled up well against the cold with boots, a warm jacket, a scarf, mittens, and a hat. Get yourself a snow shovel and head outside. You're about to build something that will last until the first big thaw!

How much snow do you need to make a snowman? A lot. More than a lot. Way more than you think.

You'll need to make three spheres: one very big, one of moderate size, and one small. You'll need to pack the snow together as much as possible, compressing it until it's nice and solid. That's why you need so much snow!

The biggest of your three spheres will be the base of the snowman—its belly and legs. The medium-sized one will be the chest and shoulders, and the smallest one will be the head. Place one on top of the other so they are well balanced. If they don't hold well, you can insert a stick vertically through the spheres, making a sort of spine for the snowman.

Now your snowman needs arms, made from two twigs, and a face. In cartoons, they always use a carrot for the nose, two pieces of coal for the eyes, and an old hat to provide shelter from the wind.

What will you use for the mouth? And what name will you give your snowman?

✓ MISSION ACCOMPLISHED!

🏆 MY POINTS FOR THIS ADVENTURE:

(score each category from 1 to 10)

Courage: _____

Curiosity/interest: _____

Care/attention: _____

Success/achievement: _____

Fun: _____

WHAT YOU'LL REMEMBER MOST ABOUT THIS ADVENTURE:

The cold, the whiteness of the snow, and the effort it took to give shape to a mountain of snowflakes.

RECOMMENDED READING:

Odd and the Frost Giants
by Neil Gaiman

BUILD AN IGLOO

It's easier than you think to build a shelter like those used by the Inuit (a small Arctic population that lives in an icy climate all year long). The basic raw material is snow, just like in Adventure #24. You might want to do both of these together.

First, make your bricks of snow, pressing and forming them so they're solid. If you want, you can use a shovel or a box to help give the bricks their shape.

You'll then place your bricks in a circle, one right next to another. There will be some empty gaps, which you can pack with loose snow. Then, put on your second layer of snow bricks, this one moved a tiny bit closer to the middle of your circle. Keep building up your layers of bricks, nudging each new layer a little closer to the middle of the circle so you're closing the structure bit by bit, as it gets built up.

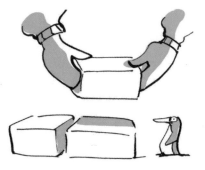

When you get to the peak of your igloo, create a round piece of pressed snow to use as your "roof." Does your igloo stay standing? Excellent—it's time to open the door and go out.

Trace an arch in the wall of the igloo that's big enough for you to crawl through. Use a stick to cut the snow out of the arch and throw it aside. Inuit protect themselves from the wind by building a little entrance tunnel out of snow. But you don't need to.

Your igloo is complete. How will you furnish it?

 MISSION ACCOMPLISHED!

Make a sketch of your igloo here so you don't forget what it looked like. If it came out a little crooked, don't worry—imperfections make things more interesting.

 **MY POINTS FOR THIS ADVENTURE:**

(score each category from 1 to 10)

Courage: _____

Curiosity/interest: _____

Care/attention: _____

Success/achievement: _____

Fun: _____

RECOMMENDED READING:

The Inuit: Ivory Carvers of the Far North

by Rachel A. Koestler-Grack

WHAT YOU'LL REMEMBER MOST ABOUT THIS ADVENTURE:

Your cheeks burning from the cold, the cold snow biting your hands, your igloo taking shape one brick at a time, your shouts of joy when you completed the project...and when you realized you shut yourself inside.

GO SLEDDING

Remember the hill from Adventure #19? Go back there in winter with a sled and have a fun, slippery, exciting ride down it!

If you don't have a sled, you can also use a bobsled or an inflatable "doughnut" tire. Even a big piece of cardboard will work. The important thing is that you're covered and well padded from head to toe to protect yourself if you wipe out.

And if sliding down the hill seems too easy to you, take a shovel and make a ramp or ski jump with a big pile of snow. Pack the snow down so it's nice and firm. You'll need to build it near the bottom of the hill (so you can reach maximum speed).

And now, go for it! How fast can you go? How far will you be able to fly?

✓ MISSION ACCOMPLISHED!

 MY POINTS FOR THIS ADVENTURE:

(score each category from 1 to 10)

Courage: _____

Curiosity/interest: _____

Care/attention: _____

Success/achievement: _____

Fun: _____

WHAT YOU'LL REMEMBER MOST ABOUT THIS ADVENTURE:

The icy wind that smacked your face, your labored breathing as you climbed back up the hill, and the spills from landings that ended badly.

RECOMMENDED READING:

Snow Treasure
by Marie McSwigan

GO TO BATTLE

To fight a true battle, you need a big group of people: the more, the better. Going into battle awakens your primitive instincts, taking you back to a time when leaving your cave each day meant risking your life. During battle, your senses get sharper, you see and hear better, and you notice movements and sounds that you might not under normal circumstances. And it's not just your brain functioning at a high level: your heart beats wildly, pumping blood and adrenaline to all of your muscles. *Run!* it says, and your muscles prepare to obey. *Look out! It's a trap!* it shouts, and you jump to avoid the danger. Attack and be attacked. Hit and be hit.

But no one really gets hurt, and when it's all over you're still good friends.

Special Rules for Battle:

Don't ever hit others with the intention of hurting them.

Stop as soon as someone asks to stop.

Recognize when someone is in trouble and help them.

The Winter Battle:

The most incredible battle you can have in the winter is a snowball fight. Wait until after a big snowfall and then make plans with your friends to meet up in an area with a wide-open space. This can be an empty parking lot, a field, or a playground. Count out and divide the group into at least two teams (see the appendix on choosing sides), spread out, and give yourselves fifteen minutes to build your respective snow forts.

Your forts are your places of safety, where you are protected from enemy attacks. One of your forts can be home base, where whoever is inside can't be hit by someone from the other side. The forts are off-limits—they can't be destroyed by snowballs (therefore, no attacks and no charging through them). They must be tall enough to completely protect you when you're crouched down, and wide enough for two or three teammates to fit in.

Then, you need to prepare the snowballs. You'll need a lot of snowballs that you can stack behind your forts in a stockpile. They should fit neatly in your hand, ready to be thrown. You need to pack them a little, but not so much that they get as hard as a rock. You're throwing them to hit someone, not hurt someone—otherwise, the battle is over. But the only other rules are these: Hit the other team with snowballs, but avoid hitting the forts. Whoever gets hit should pretend to be "out" and leave the game, but don't count on that. It's more likely they will ignore that rule and keep playing until all the snow melts. And don't worry if someone new sees you fighting and wants to join the battle—the biggest snowball fight ever fought took place in Seattle between 5,834 people.

If it's summer, you can challenge your friends to a battle with water guns and water balloons. Or, whether it's winter or summer, you can find an empty garage or room in the house and try a pillow fight. You have to remember only one thing: the special rules apply to all battles!

✔ MISSION ACCOMPLISHED!

Number of forts created:

1. _____
2. _____
3. _____
4. _____
5. _____
6. _____
7. _____

🏆 MY POINTS FOR THIS ADVENTURE:

(score each category from 1 to 10)

Courage: _____

Curiosity/interest: _____

Care/attention: _____

Success/achievement: _____

Fun: _____

WHAT YOU'LL REMEMBER MOST ABOUT THIS ADVENTURE:

The need to move so fast that you didn't even have time to think, being hit when you least expected it, and a ton of laughs. Seriously, a ton.

RECOMMENDED READING:

The Wednesday Wars
by Gary D. Schmidt

GO FOSSIL HUNTING

Let's put things in perspective: You are less than fourteen years old. TV was invented about one hundred years ago. America was discovered about five hundred years ago. Writing was invented about five thousand years ago. Fossils trace back to at least two billion years ago. Earth was created approximately 4.54 billion years ago. Fossils are the petrified remains of living things: dinosaurs, shellfish, flowers, seeds, and even single-celled organisms (those that are made of only one cell, like certain algae and fungi). They are snapshots of a faraway time—so far away that it's difficult to imagine.

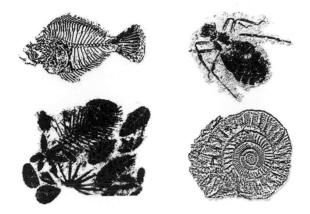

The formation of a fossil is very rare. After the living thing dies, specific conditions need to be met so that decomposition does not begin. When those conditions occur, rather than rotting and disintegrating, the organic material petrifies and stays underground for millions of years, waiting for someone to discover it. That someone could be you!

To complete this Adventure, you have to have a camera (a cell phone works too) and you need to find a place where fossils are found in rocks. You can typically find them on "split hills" (that is, hills that have been cut by landslides or excavation), on the banks of rivers rich with sedimentary rocks (that is, those that are eroded by wind and water), in caves, and on rarely used beaches.

Find at least one fossil and take a photo, but don't take the fossil with you. Fossils are rare and delicate, and they should be left where you find them.

 MISSION ACCOMPLISHED!

The fossil that I found looked like this:

MY POINTS FOR THIS ADVENTURE:

(score each category from 1 to 10)

Courage: _____

Curiosity/interest: _____

Care/attention: _____

Success/achievement: _____

Fun: _____

WHAT YOU'LL REMEMBER MOST ABOUT THIS ADVENTURE:

Looking at something that lived long ago.

RECOMMENDED READING:

Dinosaur Boy
by Cory Putman Oakes

ADVENTURE #29

FORM A SECRET CLUB

No one needs to know that you are working on this Adventure—no one.

Read these pages in secret—maybe in bed under the covers with only a flashlight or hidden in a tree like in Adventure #9.

A secret club isn't a joke. If you want it to TRULY be secret, you need to use all of the necessary precautions to keep it hidden. It takes only one false step for the club to be discovered, and suddenly everyone will know about it.

Talk with some friends about your interest in starting the club. They should be friends you trust—really, your most trusted friends in the world.

People who you'd trust with your life. You can talk to them at school about it, but that's risky. Someone might overhear. It's better to talk at someone's house where you know you won't be overheard.

Elect a president who the others will listen to and who can be in charge of voting. Things in the club will be decided by a majority.

On your agenda, put the following:

1. Choose a club name. It should be a name that's full of mystery and intrigue. It doesn't matter if no one outside the club ever learns the name. You, the members of the secret club, will know what it is.
2. Draft your list of rules. Write down what the goals of the club will be. For example: to clean up the neighborhood, raise money for a good cause, or help someone who's in trouble. Vote on the goals in a meeting, and write in the rules the ones that were voted in. At the end of the list of rules, all the members should sign their names. The president should keep the list of rules in a safe place.
3. Write the oath. To enter the club, members have to take an oath. It should be done roughly like this: "I solemnly swear to respect the laws of the club, to maintain the secrecy of my membership and that of the others, and do my best to work on our goals. Let my tongue fall out if I am lying." The oath should be read with all the members present.
4. Design your membership cards. These are like your ID cards. Get some pieces of cardboard the size of a business card and

write the name of club on them. Then, write in the name of the member and "SECRET MEMBER" on it.

5. Decide on your secret word. This word will be used for access to your hideout (if you have one) or your secret meetings.

As part of your club's activities, you could complete the Adventures in this book. Share the book with the other members. Organize a treasure hunt for nonmembers (Adventure #7) to see if they should join your club or sleep as a group in a dangerous place (Adventure #11). Trust each other and help each other. Do great things together.

✅ MISSION ACCOMPLISHED!

MY POINTS FOR THIS ADVENTURE:
(score each category from 1 to 10)

Courage: _____

Curiosity/interest: _____

Care/attention: _____

Success/achievement: _____

Fun: _____

WHAT YOU'LL REMEMBER MOST ABOUT THIS ADVENTURE:

Making all the decisions about the club name and goals, and the evenings you spent together completing an Adventure.

RECOMMENDED READING:

Harry Potter and the Order of the Phoenix by J. K. Rowling

ADVENTURE #30

WRITE A SECRET MESSAGE

Did you establish your secret club in Adventure #29?

Now you need a system for communicating secretly with your club's members. Text messages don't count! There is always the risk that your cell phone could end up in the wrong hands.

The need to send secret messages has always existed. Think about generals who needed to send orders to their officers during battle: the enemy could not know what those orders were, or they'd easily win.

Here's an interesting method: Caesar's Codebook. It's called that because Julius Caesar used this method. With it, you can make any message impossible for anyone to read who doesn't have the key to decipher it.

Look at this table:

A	B	C	D	E	F	G	H	I	J	K	L	M	N	O	P	Q	R	S	T	U	V	W	X	Y	Z
E	F	G	H	I	J	K	L	M	N	O	P	Q	R	S	T	U	V	W	X	Y	Z	A	B	C	D

Do you notice something peculiar?

The second line is in alphabetical order, but the letters are advanced four spots. Many people only use one or two letters forward, but we don't want Caesar or his insiders to be able to read our messages, so we changed it.

This is how you'll code your message:

1. Write your message (e.g., SEE YOU LATER).
2. Using the table, substitute each letter for the corresponding letter in the lower row (e.g., WII CSY PEXIV).
3. Send the message to someone in your secret club.

Do you get how it works? **Try to decode this message:**

IBGIPPIRX CSY HMH MX.

Do you want to make an even more complicated code? Randomly mix up the letters of the second row. Only those who have the same table as you will be able to decode your messages!

✔ MISSION ACCOMPLISHED!

Write a secret message that only
you and your club can decode.

MY POINTS FOR THIS ADVENTURE:

(score each category from 1 to 10)

Courage: _____

Curiosity/interest: _____

Care/attention: _____

Success/achievement: _____

Fun: _____

WHAT YOU'LL REMEMBER MOST ABOUT THIS ADVENTURE:

Watching what looked like a lot of random letters becoming, letter by letter, a message that made complete sense.

RECOMMENDED READING:

The Mysterious Benedict Society
by Trenton Lee Stewart

ADVENTURE #31

TRAIL A FRIEND
WITHOUT THEM KNOWING IT

I t's impossible to hide it: trailing someone is one of the least exciting activities one can undertake. You need a ton of patience, you spend a lot of time on your feet, and you usually don't learn anything interesting anyway.

But surveillance is one of the oldest and most important activities that Adventurers undertake, and members of a secret club should know how it's done.

Trailing someone consists of following someone and finding out where they go and who they meet. The subject must not realize they're being followed, or your efforts will be wasted.

1. Choose someone to follow who you know—maybe a classmate. Don't choose a stranger.
2. Don't lose sight of the person, but make sure they don't see you.
3. Always stay behind the person. Wear a hat or cap so you can put it on and take it off every once in a while. It's sort of a disguise.
4. Take a notebook with you so you can write down what your subject does and who talks with them. Remember to write down the precise time. For example: *At 1:11 p.m.—The subject went to the ice-cream store. He bought a double scoop cone. It looked like he chose chocolate.*
5. When you have discovered where your subject went, you can check off this Adventure from your list.

✅ MISSION ACCOMPLISHED!

I followed (full name):

_____

and discovered that the person went to (address):

_____

I also learned:

_____

_____

_____

🏆 MY POINTS FOR THIS ADVENTURE:

(score each category from 1 to 10)

Courage: _____

Curiosity/interest: _____

Care/attention: _____

Success/achievement: _____

Fun: _____

WHAT YOU'LL REMEMBER MOST ABOUT THIS ADVENTURE:

Learning something new about your friend and making sure that no one followed you.

RECOMMENDED READING:

Harriet the Spy
by Louise Fitzhugh

EXPLORE A MYSTERIOUS OLD RUIN

Have you noticed that old house on the hill? It's said to be inhabited by ghosts. The lighthouse on the point? In the darkest nights, the light goes on in the watchtower. That crumbling farmhouse in the woods? Demons have been seen wandering around over there.

These are phenomena that no one can explain, but are intriguing and mysterious.

To complete this Adventure, you need to explore a mysterious ruin.

Here are some safety suggestions: Abandoned buildings are extremely dangerous. The many years of neglect have weakened their structure, and it might be that your weight could be enough to make a floor fall in. Always walk close to the wall of a building where the floor is the strongest or don't actually enter the building if it looks like it's falling apart. If you see dust or mold, hold your breath and get out right away. It could be harmful to your health.

Make sure you get your parent or guardian's permission. Move carefully and don't go alone. Keep some friends within earshot. Bring a flashlight and make sure someone at home knows where you went. Feel free to take photos. Who knows? The flash might capture something that escaped the naked eye...

Happy ghost hunting!

✓ MISSION ACCOMPLISHED!

The most mysterious things
I saw:

🏆 **MY POINTS FOR THIS ADVENTURE:**

(score each category from 1 to 10)

Courage: _____

Curiosity/interest: _____

Care/attention: _____

Success/achievement: _____

Fun: _____

WHAT YOU'LL REMEMBER MOST ABOUT THIS ADVENTURE:

The danger, the risk, and the unmistakable smell of something old and abandoned.

RECOMMENDED READING:

Dial-a-Ghost by Eva Ibbotson

IMITATE A FAMOUS PERSON FROM HISTORY

History isn't just dates, places, and facts. More than anything, history is made up of the hopes and dreams and hard work of real men and women.

Choose a historical figure that you admire: Marie Curie, Frida Kahlo, Leonardo da Vinci, Joan of Arc, Nelson Mandela, or someone like that.

Find out everything you can about this person. Where were they born? What was their family like? Discover what they did that made them famous. Imagine what that person was like when they were your age. Investigate their history and life story.

If your person was a writer, read something that they wrote

that you haven't read before. If your person was an artist, learn the details about one of their most famous works of art. If your person was an inventor, find out how one of their inventions changed the world.

Then, put yourself in their shoes and imagine you are that person.

For example, did you know that Julius Caesar talked about himself in the third person? "He liked this pork pie very much." Try to talk like Caesar for a whole day: "This cereal is very good. She will eat all of it." Or: "He does not wish to do his homework. He will go play in the backyard."

Over the next few days, take some time to try to act like the person you chose. At the end of it, answer these questions: What was it like to be that person? What do you think made them great? Why are they considered a part of history? And how can you do something just as great?

✓ MISSION ACCOMPLISHED!

For several days I lived like
(name of the historical figure that you chose):

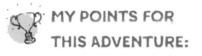 **MY POINTS FOR
THIS ADVENTURE:**

(score each category from 1 to 10)

Courage: _____

Curiosity/interest: _____

Care/attention: _____

Success/achievement: _____

Fun: _____

**WHAT YOU'LL
REMEMBER MOST
ABOUT THIS ADVENTURE:**

Knowing so much more about a historical figure than when you started the Adventure.

RECOMMENDED READING:

Eleanor Roosevelt: A Life of Discovery by Russell Freedman

ADVENTURE #34

NORTH

WEST

EAST

SOUTH

FIND YOUR WAY WITH
A COMPASS AND MAP

Compasses and maps have always been the valued tools of traveling explorers. They've helped prevent Adventurers from taking the wrong paths or roads and ending up getting lost. And for those few courageous explorers that have gone where no one else had been before, updating existing maps and creating new maps was their most important responsibility. The compass is the instrument that always indicates where north is. It's a map's best friend, and you should learn how to use it.

To complete this Adventure, you need to get a map of a

place you don't know that's not far from home (otherwise you won't be able to get there), a compass (if you don't have one at home, you can try sports or outdoor equipment stores), and an adventurous spirit.

(You can download a printed map from the internet.)

This Adventure consists of you walking one hundred steps north and two hundred steps east. A good place for this activity is a park or an open field.

This is how you'll do it:

Choose a starting point, spread out your map on the ground or on a flat surface, and lay your compass on it.

The top edge of the map will be north, and the bottom will be south. To determine where north is, you need to set the compass next to the map and wait until the compass needle is pointed to the north. Then, turn the map until the top of the map is facing the same direction as the compass needle. North is the direction you'll be walking.

While you're walking, place the compass in the palm of your hand and keep your hand in front of your chest. This is the correct position for using a compass while moving. After you've walked one hundred steps north, look at which direction the needle is pointing at for east. Turn in that direction and walk two hundred steps and see where you end up.

Happy exploring!

✔ MISSION ACCOMPLISHED!

Departure point:
_____

_____

Arrival point:
_____

_____

🏆 MY POINTS FOR THIS ADVENTURE:

(score each category from 1 to 10)

Courage: _____

Curiosity/interest: _____

Care/attention: _____

Success/achievement: _____

Fun: _____

WHAT YOU'LL REMEMBER MOST ABOUT THIS ADVENTURE:

The moment you finished walking and figured out where you were on the printed map.

RECOMMENDED READING:

The Map to Everywhere by Carrie Ryan and John Parke Davis

WRITE A NEWSLETTER OR BLOG

Once upon a time, knowing something that was happening on the other side of the world was not easy. News traveled by foot or on the back of a donkey, by way of merchants or aristocrats. It used to take months for news to spread.

Today, it's possible to communicate in real time with any other place in the world, including the South Pole. Satellite communications ensure that talking to your neighbor or chatting with a sailor in the middle of the ocean are equally possible. With a click, you can know what's happening in Hong Kong or watch emperor penguins in New Zealand online.

But who shares all of this information? Who decides what's worth mentioning and what isn't? That job belongs to journalists. They learn about things and then write about them so others can know what's happening around the world. In some ways, a journalist is like a detective; they have to investigate facts and then tell people about what they've discovered.

To complete this Adventure, you have to write a newsletter or blog. This is a fun project, and you may want to get your class involved if your teacher thinks it's a good idea. You can also try this with your secret club from Adventure #29.

You can choose anything to be the topic of your newsletter. You could gather news about your school, friends, or neighborhood.

To begin, you can read magazines or newspapers for inspiration and to become familiar with the writing style. Then, get informed about the topic you want to tackle. You need to know it thoroughly so you can describe it to others. When interviewing someone, ask detailed, researched questions and listen intently. Only some of what you hear will end up in your article, but the final result will be rich and complete.

If you prefer, instead of a newsletter, you can start a blog online (though you must get your parents' or guardian's permission). A blog is a type of diary or journal that others can read, but instead of writing it on paper, you write it online. You can write a blog about how you're completing the Adventures in this book and even show some pictures from the work you've done.

Don't be afraid of the technical aspects. Having a blog is super simple, and you don't even have to be that great at using a computer. You can start by joining one of many free blog hosting services on the web and be online within a half hour.

Once you've started your newsletter or blog, you have to keep it active. That means you have to post new articles at least once each week.

Here are some topic ideas:
- Video games
- Sports
- Music
- Movies

 MISSION ACCOMPLISHED!

MY POINTS FOR THIS ADVENTURE:

(score each category from 1 to 10)

Courage: _____

Curiosity/interest: _____

Care/attention: _____

Success/achievement: _____

Fun: _____

WHAT YOU'LL REMEMBER MOST ABOUT THIS ADVENTURE:

New discoveries, new friends, and comments from readers.

RECOMMENDED READING:

Dear Opl by Shelley Sackier

MAKE IT TO THE END
OF A DIFFICULT VIDEO GAME

Have you ever played all the way to the end of a video game? You need dedication, concentration, and determination. Long hours of training might be necessary, as well as careful planning and many, many attempts.

To complete this Adventure, you have to make it to the final level of a video game—it doesn't matter which one.

It's best if it's a game you're excited to play.

Gaming consoles and old games:

To choose your game, you don't have to spend a lot of money. The best games today are those from apps that cost less than $10. You can also try old video games from many years ago that are no longer on the market but that you can find and download online.

These are called *retro games*, and you can play them online. You can attempt this challenge with *The Legend of Zelda, Ghosts 'n Goblins, Black Tiger, Project Firestart, Monkey Island, Tomb Raider,* and *Zak McKracken and the Alien Mindbenders*. But there are thousands to choose from—enough to keep you busy for years.

 **MISSION ACCOMPLISHED!**

🏆 **MY POINTS FOR THIS ADVENTURE:**

(score each category from 1 to 10)

Courage: _____

Curiosity/interest: _____

Care/attention: _____

Success/achievement: _____

Fun: _____

RECOMMENDED READING:

Secret Coders by Gene Luen Yang and Mike Holmes

WHAT YOU'LL REMEMBER MOST ABOUT THIS ADVENTURE:

The challenge of having to start repeatedly and the thrill of being the best in the world when you finally arrived at the end.

CREATE A FRIENDLY MONSTER

Who isn't scared of monsters? At the same time, who doesn't love monsters? Monsters are everywhere. Some are super scary, like those that hide under the bed. Others are a little less scary, and they make us laugh. If, like most of us, you're scared of but fascinated by monsters, the best way to get to know them is to complete this Adventure, which requires you to make a monster.

How do you make a monster? It's not enough just to imagine one—you have to actually build one. You could make one by stacking cardboard boxes and painting a monster's face and body, collecting special rocks and painting your monster's face, or sculpting a monster with modeling clay.

If you don't have modeling clay, you can make your own from scratch. Mix together 1 cup of water, 1 cup of salt, 1 cup of flour, 1 teaspoon of wood glue, and 1 teaspoon of cooking oil. You'll be able to sculpt with this mixture, and it should dry into something solid that doesn't fall apart.

The important thing about this Adventure is to create a monster that is really, really personal— so personal that, when you're done, you give it a name and decide what its purpose is. Does it protect you? Watch over your secret hideout? Or guard your favorite treasures?

Think about it for a while before you begin to create your monster, because once it's done, it's done.

✓ MISSION ACCOMPLISHED!

Draw the monster you created below:

🏆 **MY POINTS FOR THIS ADVENTURE:**

(score each category from 1 to 10)

Courage: _____

Curiosity/interest: _____

Care/attention: _____

Success/achievement: _____

Fun: _____

WHAT YOU'LL REMEMBER MOST ABOUT THIS ADVENTURE:

Something you created with your own two hands—a unique monster no one has thought of before.

RECOMMENDED READING:

Scary Stories to Tell in the Dark
by Alvin Schwartz

ADVENTURE #38

INVENT A MAGIC POTION

S nail slime, powdered sugar, earthworms...any ingredients can be used to create a magic potion or witches' brew.

If you could invent a magic potion, how would you do it? Would it be colorful and perfumed, or smelly and disgusting? What would the ingredients be—most importantly, what would its magical purpose be?

Take a large container and combine your ingredients to make a magical liquid. (Don't use anything with chemical ingredients, like household cleaning products.) Mix your potion together really well, and then make your friends smell it and ask them to guess the ingredients. The potion is for smelling only—nobody should drink it!

When you're finished, you can put the potion in a bottle with a screw top to seal it—or you can pour the potion down the sink and move on to another Adventure. Whatever you do, be sure not to leave your potion out in the open for a witch to find.

✓ MISSION ACCOMPLISHED!

The secret ingredients of my potion were:

1. _____
2. _____
3. _____
4. _____
5. _____
6. _____
7. _____

🏆 MY POINTS FOR THIS ADVENTURE:

(score each category from 1 to 10)

Courage: _____

Curiosity/interest: _____

Care/attention: _____

Success/achievement: _____

Fun: _____

WHAT YOU'LL REMEMBER MOST ABOUT THIS ADVENTURE:

The changing color of the potion as you added new ingredients and the strange smells you created.

RECOMMENDED READING:

The Witches by Roald Dahl

WRITE A STORY

It's pretty easy to tell when a story is great—you race to the end and are sad when it's over. But people don't realize how hard it can be to create a story from scratch.

There's no magic formula for writing a satisfying story, but here are some tips that will help.

First, you need a main character who has some interesting story to tell. Your character can be totally normal, without any special talents, but then something extraordinary needs to happen to them that changes their life. (Harry Potter, for example, thought he was an average kid and had no idea about his hidden magic.)

The next step is to imagine a special event or challenge for your main character. It could be an huge problem—an extremely difficult assignment that requires a lot of thought to solve.

One of the twelve labors of Hercules was to clean the immense stables of Augeas in only one day. This was an impossible task even for a quick and strong guy like him. But Hercules changed the course of a river so that it swept through the stables, clearing them of all traces of dirt and grime.

Good stories, at their core, are like that. We want to see how a character solves their problems.

If you try this Adventure, don't get discouraged if you have trouble coming up with ideas at first. That's normal. You need to think a lot about the plot and concentrate without getting too distracted.

When you've written your story, put it in a drawer for a week. Forget about it and think about other things. Then, read it again. It may seem like someone else wrote it. You'll probably see some things that you want to change. Or maybe you'll find that it's too long and needs to be edited. When you're finally satisfied with it, give it to someone else to read—or publish it in your newsletter or blog from Adventure #35.

✅ MISSION ACCOMPLISHED!

🏆 MY POINTS FOR THIS ADVENTURE:

(score each category from 1 to 10)

Courage: _____

Curiosity/interest: _____

Care/attention: _____

Success/achievement: _____

Fun: _____

WHAT YOU'LL REMEMBER MOST ABOUT THIS ADVENTURE:

The challenge of looking at a blank page and then seeing the finished story.

RECOMMENDED READING:

The Stories Julian Tells
by Ann Cameron

ADVENTURE #40

WRITE A LETTER

Snail mail may have declined in popularity since the invention of the Internet and email, but getting a letter from a friend is still a wonderful thing. Opening an envelope is a special experience, like opening a box that contains treasures and mysteries. In addition to the letter, there might be newspaper clippings, photos, or drawings. Anything that is very thin or made from paper can be easily be sent by mail. So why not choose someone and send them a letter?

Do you have a friend or someone from your family who lives far away? Why don't you write them a nice letter?

Pay attention to details. Tell them what you're doing. Tell them anything new, different, or exciting that has happened to you recently. You can even tell them about this book and about the experiences you are having. Add drawings, a joke, a candy wrapper, or even some comic strips that you've drawn. Print some of your photos and include them. Every additional item makes the letter more memorable and special.

And if your friend or family member lives in a different country, even better: the long time it takes for mail to arrive makes it more exciting. In your letter, ask the other person to write back to you in the same way you wrote to them.

When you get their response, you'll have completed this Adventure.

The one condition for this Adventure is that your letter must be mailed and not given to the other person face-to-face. Imagine how surprised the other person will be when they get a letter from you.

✓ MISSION ACCOMPLISHED!

 MY POINTS FOR THIS ADVENTURE:

(score each category from 1 to 10)

Courage: _____

Curiosity/interest: _____

Care/attention: _____

Success/achievement: _____

Fun: _____

RECOMMENDED READING:

A Year in the Life of a Total and Complete Genius

by Stacey Matson

 **WHAT YOU'LL REMEMBER MOST ABOUT THIS ADVENTURE:**

The things you thought about before sitting down and writing your letter, mailing your letter at a post office or a mailbox, and knowing it was going to travel miles away.

ADVENTURE #41

GET SOAKED IN A RAINSTORM

Thunderstorms are loud and exciting. In ancient times, people imagined that lightning was thrown down by the gods (like Zeus) and thunder was caused by magic hammers (Thor, the god of thunder from Nordic mythology, actually carried a hammer so he could shatter mountains).

Are you sometimes scared of storms? Well, there's a way to conquer that fear.

If you go outside in the pouring rain, you might find that rainstorms can be really fun. It can be exciting to feel the sky opening up: water running down your cheeks, clothes getting drenched, and hair getting soaked.

But be careful—don't play outside in a rainstorm if there's thunder or lightning.

 MISSION ACCOMPLISHED!

Squeezing out the clothes that I wore during the storm would have filled the bucket up to here (mark up to where):

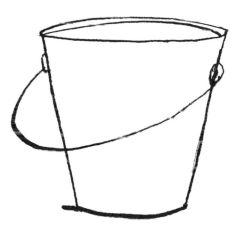

 MY POINTS FOR THIS ADVENTURE:

*(score each category from 1 to 10)

Courage: _____

Curiosity/interest: _____

Care/attention: _____

Success/achievement: _____

Fun: _____

WHAT YOU'LL REMEMBER MOST ABOUT THIS ADVENTURE:

The excitement of doing something new and feeling rain all over your skin.

RECOMMENDED READING:

Weather by Seymour Simon

ADVENTURE #42

MAKE A PLAYLIST

Choose a song, close your eyes, and listen closely to the sound. What do you think about when you hear the music? What images do you see? Are they things that you think about every day, or are they pictures from a place far away?

These questions show how music is a part of your life. It can change you from being sad to feeling happy. Maybe you use music to help you wake up in the morning. For Albert Einstein, for example, music was something he listened to help him think.

To complete this Adventure, you have to put together a playlist.

Choose a theme, like "ten songs that are about traveling" or "ten songs that have a guitar solo." Decide according to your tastes and interests. Then, select the songs. Consider each one carefully. They should work well together and have special meaning for you. Even the order you put the songs in is important.

Finally, share your playlist with your friends. You can also share it on your blog from Adventure #35.

What do your friends think? What were their favorite songs? Did they suggest other songs? Why?

✅ MISSION ACCOMPLISHED!

Here is my playlist:

🏆 MY POINTS FOR THIS ADVENTURE:

(score each category from 1 to 10)

Courage: _____

Curiosity/interest: _____

Care/attention: _____

Success/achievement: _____

Fun: _____

WHAT YOU'LL REMEMBER MOST ABOUT THIS ADVENTURE:

Taking the time to pick the right songs and making an unforgettable playlist.

RECOMMENDED READING:

Hip Hop Speaks to Children: A Celebration of Poetry with a Beat edited by Nikki Giovanni

ADVENTURE #43

PRODUCE A PLAY

How would you feel if you were the king or queen of Scotland? How would you act if you were Apollo, the son of Zeus? How would you walk if you weren't a human, but a dragon? A giant? A bird?

Acting onstage helps you answer all of these questions.

To complete this Adventure,

you need to produce a play. It can be made up of only one person (in which case it's called a monologue), or you can gather all your friends and perform a more complicated story.

You can invent your own story (and also complete Adventure #39), or you can perform the story of a person from history (taking a clue from Adventure #33) or from a book you liked.

The play shouldn't be improvised. Instead you must:

• Write the script. The script will contain all the dialogue that the actors will speak. It also includes stage directions that describe the setting of the play and directions for the actors.

• Prepare costumes. Decide on what each character should wear, and then borrow, sew, or buy what's needed.

• Paint the set. Get a huge piece of paper or an old bedsheet and paint it with the background setting of the story: a castle, if it's a knight's adventure tale; a forest, if it's a story about elves and gnomes; and so on.

• Choose the background music.

• Find a place to rehearse.

• Make sure the actors memorize their lines.

• Stage your play once everything's ready. Find a location where you can put up your set, find chairs or cushions for your audience, and choose someone from the group who can turn the music on at the right time.

If you put in enough work, you'll succeed in entertaining your audience. And you'll see that, when their applause begins, you'll feel rewarded for all your hard work.

✓ MISSION ACCOMPLISHED!

Title of the play and members
of the theater company:

🏆 MY POINTS FOR THIS ADVENTURE:

(score each category from 1 to 10)

Courage: _____

Curiosity/interest: _____

Care/attention: _____

Success/achievement: _____

Fun: _____

RECOMMENDED READING:

Dara Palmer's Major Drama
by Emma Shevah

WHAT YOU'LL REMEMBER MOST ABOUT THIS ADVENTURE:

Learning how to memorize lines, conquering your stage fright, working with the other actors as a team, and the cheers from the audience at the end of the performance.

ADVENTURE #44

BAKE BREAD (AND EAT IT)

It's time to make a mess in the kitchen.

Have you ever made something to eat? No, peeling an apple isn't considered preparing a meal. However, making a sandwich is fun to do. Some even consider it an art.

This Adventure challenges you to make bread. It's easy, fun, and, most importantly, delicious.

Did you know that ancient Greeks considered bread to be the food of the gods? They even invented a word to describe everything that you can put in bread: *companatico*. That means "with bread."

The recipe:

Gather these ingredients:

- ¼ cup of water
- 2¼ teaspoons of brewer's yeast (you can substitute 2¼ teaspoons baking powder)
- 1¼ cup of white flour
- 1¼ cup of all-purpose flour
- ¼ cup of olive oil
- 2 teaspoons of salt
- a pinch of sugar

1. Dissolve the yeast in a bowl with ¼ cup of warm water and add the pinch of sugar. If the yeast is fresh, this will activate it and create a clear foam.
2. Sift all of the flours onto a cutting board. Heap it into a mound with a hole in the middle, as if it were a volcano.
3. Slowly pour the bowl of water and yeast into the volcano, then cover the hole with a little flour.
4. Take the 1¼ cup of water. Add the oil and salt to it and mix well. Pour it all into the mountain of flour.
5. Now the most challenging step: you have to mix the dough.
6. Work the dough with your hands. Press, push, rotate, and turn the mixture. Do this for about ten minutes, until the dough is solid, elastic, and hardly sticky. If it's sticky, flour your hands and work the dough a little more.

7. Now the dough has to rise. Put it in a big bowl, cover the bowl with plastic wrap, and let it rest for a couple of hours.

8. Once the dough has doubled in size, put it on a baking sheet lined with a piece of parchment paper. Now is the time to shape your loaf. You can make a round loaf and use a knife to make an "X" on top, or you can make it long and thin like a French baguette.

9. Let the bread rise for another hour and you'll see how it doubles in size again.

10. At that point, turn the oven on to 395 degrees Fahrenheit. Put your loaf in the oven and let it bake for about forty-five minutes, until the crust becomes golden. Finally, take it out of the oven and...enjoy!

✓ MISSION ACCOMPLISHED!

 MY POINTS FOR THIS ADVENTURE:

(score each category from 1 to 10)

Courage: _____

Curiosity/interest: _____

Care/attention: _____

Success/achievement: ____

Fun: _____

RECOMMENDED READING:

The Bakery Lady/La señora de la panadería by Pat Mora and illustrated by Pablo Torecilla.

WHAT YOU'LL REMEMBER MOST ABOUT THIS ADVENTURE:

Your sticky hands, the dough that slowly transformed itself, the warm and pleasant smell of the bread baking, and the way it felt to eat that first bite of bread that you made yourself.

ADVENTURE #45

HAVE AN ADVENTURE AT THE BEACH

The world is full of sand. From fine, white sandy beaches to golden dunes, there's a lot of sand to go around. This is lucky for us, because sand is exactly what we need to complete this Adventure, which is a special Adventure in two parts.

Build a sand castle

To build a sand castle, the only thing you need is sand. Buckets and shovels help with the work, but nothing is as useful as your hands and a good amount of imagination. Dream bigger than just making walls. You can add towers, a moat, windows, and anything else you can think up.

One trick that will help you save time? Use damp sand. It is much easier to mold into shapes.

Take a sand bath

Dig a hole big enough to lie down in. Lie down in the hole and cover yourself with sand. Keep your head above the sand, and enjoy some rest and relaxation.

Sand, when it's hot, becomes sort of like an electric blanket. When you have rested enough, emerge slowly from the sand like a zombie.

This Adventure can also be considered completed if you bury a friend instead.

✔ MISSION ACCOMPLISHED!

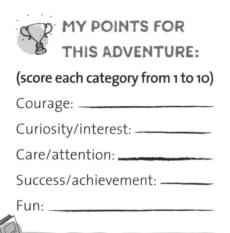 **MY POINTS FOR THIS ADVENTURE:**

(score each category from 1 to 10)

Courage: _____

Curiosity/interest: _____

Care/attention: _____

Success/achievement: _____

Fun: _____

RECOMMENDED READING:

Stringbean's Trip to the Shining Sea by Vera B. Williams and Jennifer Williams.

 WHAT YOU'LL REMEMBER MOST ABOUT THIS ADVENTURE:

Creating an amazing structure from sand, the feeling of sand all over your body, and the relief of diving into the water to wash off every tiny grain.

HAVE A MARBLE RACE

This is a fun game to play at the beach.

Some toy stores still sell marbles for racing in the sand. They are big, light, plastic marbles (the glass ones don't work well) that you push forward with a flick of a finger. If you can't find plastic marbles, choose some lightweight plastic balls.

To make the racetrack, pick a friend who doesn't weigh much and have them sit in the sand. Then, take them by the ankles and pull them through the sand, drawing a large figure eight.

You begin by having everyone line up their marbles at the starting line. After deciding what order to go in, you move your marble forward by flicking it with one finger. Each person tries to keep their marble ahead of the other players. If someone's marble goes off the track, it should be placed back at the start of that turn.

The person whose marble is in front after completing the figure eight is the winner.

✅ MISSION ACCOMPLISHED!

🏆 **MY POINTS FOR THIS ADVENTURE:**

(score each category from 1 to 10)

Courage: _____

Curiosity/interest: _____

Care/attention: _____

Success/achievement: _____

Fun: _____

RECOMMENDED READING:

The Gollywhopper Games
by Jody Feldman

WHAT YOU'LL REMEMBER MOST ABOUT THIS ADVENTURE:

The sand under your fingernails (or in your bathing suit, if you were the one who was pulled along to make the track), the cheers of the players when they had a good shot, and wanting to play again after finishing a game.

ADVENTURE #47

AN ADULT MUST BE PRESENT!

EXPLORE YOUR
OWN CITY BLINDFOLDED

Do you really know your city, town, or neighborhood?

Close your eyes and imagine being on a street—any street. Can you imagine the stores, the parked cars, and the pedestrians? Now try to imagine a place you want to walk and the route you will take to get there. Maybe it's a walk to the library or park. Maybe the walk takes you past your school or through downtown. Do you remember every turn you take to get to your destination? Do you remember the number of stop signs or whether there were any traffic lights?

Now it gets more challenging: Can you imagine the

sounds? The traffic, the other people walking past and talking on their phones, the trains and factories in the distance, and the smells?

Almost everyone can remember the places they have visited, but the sounds and other details are easier to forget.

This mission will help you discover something about your city, town, or neighborhood that you didn't know before. Are you ready?

Ask a parent to join you. Get a blindfold (a dark scarf, a sleeping mask, some cloth to wrap around your head—even a couple of pirate eye patches!) and put it on before you leave your house. You should hold on to your parent's arm at the elbow and let them guide you, helping you avoid different obstacles and keeping you safe. Your parent will decide where you will go. They could choose a street you walk on all the time or explore a part of the city that you don't know well.

You can't look, but you can listen, feel the temperature, the changes in air, and the smells. All of your other senses will be heightened because you're using them to concentrate.

✓ MISSION ACCOMPLISHED!

Write the sensations and feelings that you had during this Adventure:

🏆 MY POINTS FOR THIS ADVENTURE:

(score each category from 1 to 10)

Courage: _____

Curiosity/interest: _____

Care/attention: _____

Success/achievement: _____

Fun: _____

WHAT YOU'LL REMEMBER MOST ABOUT THIS ADVENTURE:

Discovering new things about places you thought you knew well and learning about a whole new area.

RECOMMENDED READING:

City Atlas by Georgia Cherry

ADVENTURE #48

TAKE APART AND REBUILD A TOY

We're surrounded by objects that hide complex parts and secret mechanisms that operate without being seen. The best engineers work to design cell phones, electronics, computers, action figures, and all kinds of toys.

Have you ever wondered how they work? What's inside? Good! Curiosity is the mark of an Adventurer.

Get some screwdrivers, choose a toy that interests you, and take it apart. You may want to buy an old toy to experiment with the first time. And in case you can't put it back together, don't take apart a toy that's special to you.

You might select an old-fashioned toy like a windup train or car. These toys have mechanisms, levers, and wheels.

Do not choose anything that runs on electricity or batteries.

✓ MISSION ACCOMPLISHED!

🏆 MY POINTS FOR THIS ADVENTURE:

(score each category from 1 to 10)

Courage: _____

Curiosity/interest: _____

Care/attention: _____

Success/achievement: _____

Fun: _____

WHAT YOU'LL REMEMBER MOST ABOUT THIS ADVENTURE:

Discovering all the parts used to make one toy and learning that taking a toy apart (and putting it back together) can be just as much fun as playing with it.

RECOMMENDED READING:

The Invention of Hugo Cabret by Brian Selznick

WRITE UP A LIST
OF WISHES TO COMPLETE

This is a special Adventure—one that will be challenging but rewarding.

To complete it, you have to write down a list of ten wishes. It can include both things that you wish for yourself and things you wish for your friends and family. For example, have you always dreamed of going on a plane? That could be your first wish. Would you like to help your mom or dad tackle a big cleaning project around the house? That could be your second wish. Would you like to spend the day hanging out with your best friend? That could be the third. Do you want a pet? And so on.

To complete this Adventure, you have to fulfill at least three wishes from the list and make an effort to make the other wishes come true in the years to come.

Writing down your wishes and completing them will give you a sense of accomplishment.

✔ MISSION ACCOMPLISHED!

Wishes:

🏆 **MY POINTS FOR THIS ADVENTURE:**

(score each category from 1 to 10)

Courage: —————————————

Curiosity/interest: ——————

Care/attention: ——————————

Success/achievement: ————

Fun: ———————————————

WHAT YOU'LL REMEMBER MOST ABOUT THIS ADVENTURE:

Only you can know that.

RECOMMENDED READING:

Stargirl by Jerry Spinelli

ADVENTURE #50

MAKE A TIME CAPSULE

Adventurers typically find treasures, but people often forget about the people who hid them in the first place.

To complete this final Adventure, you have to prepare a time capsule of treasures, bury it, and draw a mysterious map so that someone can find it after a long time has passed.

First and foremost, you have to decide what treasures you will hide. It should be made up of personal objects that you have used for a long time and that are important to you. It could be a comic book, a toy, or a bag of marbles. You should give up something that you think you can't live without. It's even better if you pick out more than one object. Another idea is to include a notebook filled with messages and notes from your friends and family.

Make sure to put the date on the notebook. That way whoever finds the time capsule will know when it was created.

After you have gathered everything that will be included in your time capsule, you have to find a container. The best choice is something made of tin because it's waterproof, but plastic or glass containers that you use in the kitchen (for holding food and drinks) can work as well.

This will become your time capsule—something that won't be opened for many, many years. When it's found, it will take whoever finds it back to the time you're living in right now.

The next step is to choose a special place to hide your time capsule. It could be a hole in a tree or buried in the garden. It might be deep in the bushes in your grandparents' backyard or hidden in an attic.

If you decide to dig a deep hole, you should place the time capsule at the bottom and press down firmly when you cover it with dirt.

At this point, you need to draw a map of the hiding place. Be sure to include landmarks and directions on how to find your time capsule.

Finally, hide the map. You could hide it somewhere in your room, the basement of your house, a tree house, or inside a book at the library. Someday, someone will find the map and discover your time capsule.

✅ MISSION ACCOMPLISHED!

🏆 MY POINTS FOR THIS ADVENTURE:

(score each category from 1 to 10)

Courage: _____

Curiosity/interest: _____

Care/attention: _____

Success/achievement: _____

Fun: _____

WHAT YOU'LL REMEMBER MOST ABOUT THIS ADVENTURE:

Choosing the special items to put in your time capsule, finding the perfect hiding place, and the fun of this top-secret mission.

RECOMMENDED READING:

Holes by Louis Sachar

APPENDICES

Drawing Lots

You're on a ship on a scientific mission. A gigantic octopus comes up from the depths of the ocean and attacks the boat. You have to choose some crew members who, armed with harpoons, will defend the deck. The captain lowers his bushy eyebrows and stares you in the eyes.

"You," he says with a deep voice that makes your insides twist. "You, tell me. How should I choose the volunteers?"

The captain's problem is one kids know well. Whether you play soccer, mini golf, or tennis, it's the same. You have to decide who starts, who gets the ball first, who serves first, or who chooses which side of the field they get.

If you want it to be a random decision that's fair to everyone, then you can draw lots.

The process you use depends on the number of people you have to assign to a side.

Two Players

If there are only two of you, the simplest system is to play "odds or evens."

Close your fist and say either "odds" or "evens." The other person has to choose the opposite of what you chose. Then, you chant "one-two-three!" swinging your fists to the left and the right in rhythm with the three words. At the end, you have to open your fists and make a number with your fingers. Add the two numbers (yours and the other person's) and see if the total is odd or even. The winner is the one that guesses the correct result.

If you have a coin with you, you can play heads or tails instead. As before, each person has to choose one of the options, trying to guess what the result will be. One of you tosses up the coin, flipping it in the air, and then grabs it while it's still flying and slaps it down on the back of your other hand.

That's a method that ancient Romans used, and it's still used today, all over the world. The British also play "heads or tails." Germans play "heads or numbers." Irish people play "heads or harps." In Mexico, where the Mayans and Aztecs used to live, it's "eagle or sun." Ancient Greeks played with a seashell after they had painted one side black. The game was called "day or night."

Three or More Players

Pluck as many blades of grass as there are players. The stems of weeds also work. They should all be the same length except for one, which should be a little shorter than the others. Hold the blades of grass in your fist so that no one can tell which one is the short one. Then, have your friends each pick one blade of grass, and whoever picks the shortest one wins.

What if you're indoors and don't have grass at hand?

Dice and cards can also be used for drawing lots. You just have to see who rolls the biggest number on the dice, rolling a second time if there is a tie. The same goes for cards: whoever draws the card with the highest number wins (and remember that the joker counts as one).

The rules of the game

When you're in society, and by "society" we mean "with other people," you need to act according to certain rules. We have to be honorable and fair.

We have to always keep our promises.

If we feel like cheating or "forgetting" the rules of the game so we can win, then no one will ever want to play with us.

Stopping the game

During a basketball game, the referee uses a whistle to interrupt the game and get the players' attention.

For some other games, there's a code phrase that's almost universally recognized to put a stop to the action. The phrase is "TIME OUT!" and you have to yell it while raising your hands together to make a "T" shape.

If you hear someone yell "TIME-OUT," the game stops while people check to see what's happening.

Being a good sport

Everyone loses, sooner or later, and learning how to not take it so hard and to laugh it off is one of the secrets for having fun when you play. For that reason, you should try to be a good sport. We're not talking about calling people "winners" and "losers." Instead, everyone should remember today's winners could be tomorrow's losers, and vice versa.

THE END OF THE BOOK

The word "adventurer" derives from the Latin "ad ventura" and means "that which will happen." We don't know what will happen after you have completed the 50 Adventures in this book. That's for you to discover. Did you have fun? Do you feel different? Are you still you? Are you totally the same, or is something different? If you did have fun, maybe you want to try other Adventures?

We hope so.

We hope that, once you close this book, you'll open another one. And maybe, thanks to that new book, you'll discover 50 more Adventures to try. And then another 50 and so on, always testing yourself with a new discovery, an unexpected event, or an obstacle to overcome—and doing it with courage and determination.

We hope that whatever you are doing—chasing, fixing, climbing, descending, hiding, painting, writing, thinking, inventing—you are happy, because that's the real reason to seek out adventure.

NOTES, SKETCHES, DOODLES

INDEX OF THE ADVENTURES